ITALIAN
COUNTRY COOKING
THE SECRETS OF CUCINA POVERA

FALL RIVER PRESS

New York

An Imprint of Sterling Publishing
387 Park Avenue South
New York, NY 10016

© 2007 by Loukie Werle
© 2007 by Park Street Press
© 2007 by Media21 Publishing Pty Ltd

Designer: Juliana Carpenter
Original design concept: Stephen Layfield
Photography: Alan Benson
Stylist: Mary Harris
Home economist: Claire Pietersen
Additional photography: Craig Osment, Loukie Werle.
Pages 6 (far left), 8/9, 160/161, 258/259
Lonely Planet Images/Alan Benson.
Acknowledgements: Sascha Lambeth, Gabriella Maselli,
Gill O'Brien; Ici et Là, John Williams Antiques, Mosaique Imports,
Peppergreen in Berrima, The Art of Wine & Food

This 2008 edition published in arrangement with ACP Magazines Ltd, Australia.
First published in Australia in 2007 by ACP Magazines Ltd under the title
Italian Country Cooking © ACP Magazines Limited 2007. All rights reserved.

ISBN: 978-1-4351-0126-5

Manufactured in China

6 8 10 9 7 5

ITALIAN COUNTRY COOKING

THE SECRETS OF CUCINA POVERA

LOUKIE WERLE

PHOTOGRAPHED BY ALAN BENSON

STYLED BY MARY HARRIS

FALL RIVER PRESS

New York

Contents

Introduction
What is *cucina povera*?

The inspiration for this book, although I didn't know it at the time, was in a farmhouse kitchen in Sicily. Giovanna, our hostess, prepared a huge pot of soup over an open fireplace and, as always seems to happen when cooks get together, we talked about pots and knives and ingredients, and shared our experiences of life in the kitchen. She had lived in the house for over forty years and, though her English was no better than my rudimentary Italian, we got along just fine.

All kinds of ingredients went into the pot one by one – onions, garlic, beans, vegetables – and then the last thing, one solitary sausage.

"Who's going to get the sausage?" I said.

"That's for the guest," she replied.

How fabulous, I thought. All these ingredients, and all this love and care, and then to give the one precious thing to the guest. The spirit of sharing, and the generosity of it, was something I couldn't forget.

The next impetus for a *cucina povera* cookbook came at a time when bank interest rates hiked. Someone on TV said it was going to hurt people and, because they'd be hurting financially, they wouldn't eat so well. I remember looking at the screen and thinking – hold on, they can eat a lot better. In fact, if they only know how, they can eat as well as that wise woman in her Italian kitchen. And so my *cucina povera* (pron. *koo-CHEE-nah POH-veh-rah*) book came into being.

Cucina povera – there's no adequate translation, though "the poor cook" or "country food" have something of it – is about the real food of Italy. As I wrote in my book *Splendido*, the Italians treat their food as an extension of the way they live: social, approachable and, above all, surrounded by family and the people they love. The true Italian cuisine is more likely to be found in humble trattorias, homes and farmhouses than in upmarket restaurants.

Though *povera* sounds like poverty, the point isn't just the low cost of the ingredients. Certainly they're affordable, but they achieve spectacular results. The cooking techniques are simple and often slow ("fast food" is almost always expensive). The ingredients are seasonal and therefore at their best in quality and price. And there's only a small range of elements (just a few sausages, for instance, or a simple cut of meat), so it means easy preparations. Typically they include pancetta and speck, sausages, braised meat cuts, eggs, chicken, pasta, bread, beans and legumes, seasonal vegetables and fruit, inexpensive fish and seafood.

Cucina povera isn't found only in the country; it's also typical of Italian cities. The workers of Testaccio, Rome's slaughterhouse quarter, created a tradition that's based on the cheapest cuts of meat, and methods of cooking that have influenced Roman taste for centuries.

And just in case you think my story about the single "precious" sausage means the recipes in this book are going to be too frugal for your taste, don't worry. *Cucina povera*, as you'll discover when you try it, means eating plentifully and with a warm heart. In fact, quite possibly you'll eat better than you've ever done in your life.

As a Roman proverb says: *Più se spenne e pejo se magna*. The more you spend, the worse you eat.

Pasta

Ligurian pasta soup with pesto
Minestra con pasta alla Ligure

The air in Liguria is heady with the pungent fragrance of herbs, and basil in particular. Not surprisingly, this is the birthplace of Pesto Genovese, *usually served with a flat pasta called* trenette *(lit. ribbons). Interestingly, when pesto is stirred into a soup, such as this delightful pasta soup, or a more robust minestrone, the typical addition of pinenuts is left out.*

For any pesto made ahead of time, don't add the garlic and cheeses until just before serving. Garlic and cheese start to ferment after a while. Without garlic and cheese this pesto may be refrigerated for several weeks, and frozen for several months.

Make sure you break the pasta into pieces short enough to fit into a spoon, or eating this soup could become very messy.

3 tablespoons extra virgin olive oil
½ cup finely chopped fatty speck or pancetta
4 cloves garlic, chopped
1 medium ripe tomato, peeled and chopped
½ pound long dried pasta, such as linguine or spaghetti, broken into short pieces

Pesto
approx 1½ cups firmly packed fresh basil leaves
1 clove garlic, coarsely chopped
¼ cup extra virgin olive oil
1½ tablespoons freshly grated parmesan cheese
1½ tablespoons freshly grated Pecorino Romano cheese (or use extra parmesan)

To make the pesto, rinse the basil leaves and dry thoroughly in a salad spinner. Combine the basil and garlic in a processor with 1½ tablespoons of the oil. Pulse until you have a slightly chunky sauce, but not smooth, adding the remaining oil while processing. Stop once or twice to scrape the basil off the sides. Spoon into a bowl, stir in the cheeses and season with salt. Float a slick of oil on top, until ready to use.

To make the soup, combine the oil, speck and garlic in a pan and sauté over moderate heat until speck is golden and the fat is running, without browning the garlic. Stir in tomato and 6 cups water, and bring to a boil.

Stir in linguine and a good pinch of salt, and cook until al dente. Check seasoning and remove from the heat. Stir in the pesto and serve immediately.

Serves 4-6

Linguine with ginger, garlic and chili
Linguine alla zenzero e aglio

Start an elegant dinner with this pasta, an Umbrian classic. Closely related to the Roman quintessential pasta, Spaghetti with garlic, chilies and oil (Spaghetti aglio e olio), the addition of spicy ginger makes it specifically Umbrian and somehow rather festive.

Ginger may seem an exotic ingredient in Italian cooking, but Italy embraced this rhizome many centuries ago. Genoese sailors in the Middle Ages traded ginger, as well as pepper, cloves, cinnamon and pimento, but ginger was the only of these spices they would actually consume themselves on board – it staved off scurvy during their lengthy travels. In Florence, in Tuscany, a little ginger is customarily added to Pollo alla diavola *(chicken with plenty of black pepper or chili).*

handful flat-leaf parsley, with stalks
⅓ cup extra virgin olive oil
4 large cloves garlic, finely chopped
¼ teaspoon chili flakes
1-3 tablespoons finely chopped fresh ginger
1 pound long dried pasta, such as linguine or spaghetti

Take the leaves off the parsley stalks, chop finely and set aside. Chop the tender parsley stalks and discard the tough stalks.

Combine the chopped parsley stalks, oil, garlic, chili and ginger in a pan, large enough to hold the pasta later, and cook over low heat until the mixture is very fragrant, about 5 minutes. The garlic should not color.

Meanwhile, cook the pasta in plenty of salted, boiling water until al dente. Drain, reserving a small measuring cup of the cooking water. Add the pasta to the fragrant mixture, together with the reserved chopped parsley leaves, and stir over heat for 2 minutes, adding enough of the reserved pasta cooking water to keep the mixture moist. Serve on heated plates.

Serves 6 as a starter

Orecchiette with cauliflower and anchovies
Orecchiette con cavolfiore e acciughe

Made from the humblest ingredients, but how good is this! The anchovies melt away in the sauce, but that unmistakable Italian flavor sends its fragrance wafting through your house. Always make sure the oil your anchovies are preserved in is clean-smelling and not rancid. Many a perfectly executed dish has been spoiled with rancid oil – what a waste!

good handful flat-leaf parsley, with stalks
⅓ cup extra virgin olive oil
6 large cloves garlic, chopped, not too finely
6 anchovy fillets in oil, drained
2 hot red chilies, chopped, seeds removed if you like
1 cauliflower, divided into 1-2 inch cauliflowerets
¾ pound dried orecchiette or other short dried pasta, such as penne

Pick the leaves off the parsley, chop and set aside. Finely chop the tender parsley stalks, discarding the tough stalks, and combine the chopped tender stalks with the oil, garlic, anchovies and chilies in a frying pan, large enough to hold the cauliflower and pasta later. Set over low heat and cook until the mixture is fragrant, breaking up the anchovies with a wooden spoon, about 5-10 minutes, without coloring the garlic.

Meanwhile, bring a pot of salted water to a boil, large enough to cook the pasta later. Plunge in the cauliflowerets and cook until they are crisp-tender, about 3 minutes. Scoop from the pan with a large slotted spoon and transfer to the frying pan with the oil and garlic mixture, adding a few tablespoons of the cooking water. Continue cooking over moderate heat, stirring from time to time, until cauliflower is very tender and starts to break down.

When the water in the large pot boils again, stir in the orecchiette and cook until al dente, about 11 minutes (depending on brand). Drain, reserving a small measuring cup of the cooking water. Add the pasta to the frying pan and stir well, adding the reserved chopped parsley, and enough of the cooking water to moisten. Cook another 2 minutes, then transfer to a heated serving dish and serve immediately in deep, heated plates.

Serves 4

Bavette with asparagus and breadcrumbs
Bavette con asparagi e mollica

*Using breadcrumbs (*mollica or pangrattato*) on pasta is typical of* cucina povera. *Breadcrumbs are frequently used, particularly in Sicily and the southern, poorer provinces, instead of cheese such as parmesan or Pecorino Romano, which are expensive. The breadcrumbs are dry-fried until crisp and golden. Delicious.*

1 cup fluffy breadcrumbs (see page 273)
2 bunches asparagus
¾ pound long dried pasta, such as bavette or linguine
⅓ cup extra virgin olive oil
4 cloves garlic, finely chopped
¼ cup finely chopped flat-leaf parsley
freshly squeezed juice of 1 lemon

Place the breadcrumbs in a dry frying pan over moderate heat and stir with a wooden spoon until the crumbs are crisp and golden, about 5 minutes. Set aside.

Snap the woody bottoms off the asparagus and cut the stalks diagonally into 2-inch pieces. Bring a large pot of water to a boil. Add salt and plunge in the asparagus. Cook until bright green and crisp-tender, about 3 minutes. Remove with a slotted spoon and run under cold water to stop them cooking and to "set" the color.

Return the water in the pot to a boil, add the pasta and cook until al dente.

Meanwhile, combine the oil, garlic and parsley in a pan, large enough the hold the pasta later, and cook over low heat until the garlic is fragrant, about 3 minutes, stirring frequently. Stir in the asparagus. Stir over low heat for 1-2 minutes, until the asparagus pieces are well coated.

When the pasta is just al dente, drain, but reserve a small measuring cup of the cooking water. Add the pasta to the pan containing the asparagus, together with the lemon juice. Add enough cooking water to moisten. Turn the heat up to high and toss another 1-2 minutes, adding more water if necessary. Serve in heated bowls and scatter with the reserved crumbs.

Serves 4

Orecchiette with potatoes, garlic and chicory
Orecchiette con patate, aglio e cicoria

A favorite in our house, this dish contains slightly more oil than I would normally use. The reason is the potatoes, which are cooked with the pasta. Once these are drained, they're bathed in the oil, fragrant with plenty of garlic and a small amount of chili flakes. Less oil just wouldn't coat the potatoes and pasta sufficiently.

The combination of bland potatoes and slightly bitter chicory is sensational. Try broccoli raab for an equally interesting flavor, or Swiss chard or spinach for a milder variation.

Choose a pasta which will cook to al dente (still left with a little "bite") in about 10-12 minutes, to make sure everything's ready at the same time.

4 large cloves garlic, chopped
⅓ cup extra virgin olive oil
¼ teaspoon chili flakes
1 pound waxy potatoes, cut into ¾-inch cubes
¾ pound orecchiette or other short dried pasta, such as casareccia or penne
1 large bunch chicory, tough stems removed, leaves cut into ½-inch strips

Combine the garlic, oil and chili flakes in a small frying pan and cook over very low heat until the garlic is fragrant, about 5-10 minutes. Don't let the garlic turn any darker than a light golden color.

Meanwhile, bring a large pot of water to a boil and add salt. Add the potatoes and cook 2 minutes. Add the pasta and cook until nearly al dente, timing according to directions on the package, and potatoes are tender. Add the chicory to the pot and cook just until it wilts.

Drain the pasta, potatoes and chicory, reserving a small measuring cup of the cooking water, and transfer to a heated bowl. Pour over the garlic mixture and toss well, adding a little of the cooking water to moisten, if necessary. Serve immediately in deep, heated plates.

Serves 4

Autumn
the magic of Rome

We landed in Rome early one Sunday. It was a grey morning in October, and the taxi driver whisked us at white-knuckle speed from Fiumicino to the streets beyond Piazza del Popolo, where we'd taken a house with friends.

In contrast, Rome seemed to be asleep. In its early-morning state the area didn't look very promising. The main thoroughfare thereabouts, Via Flaminia, is one of Rome's most historic trade routes, the principal link to the east for thousands of years. That Sunday morning the street was shuttered and lifeless.

It wasn't till next morning that the shutters came down from the shop windows, the iron bars slid back, the hole-in-the-wall tobacco merchant opened for business, and what we'd thought was an empty parking lot buzzed with life. It was, in fact, the Mercato Rionale, *the local market, and it was to become a favorite haunt of ours. There was a deli, a fishmonger selling fabulous Adriatic clams, a butcher, a mini-supermarket and a laundry.*

And – a great discovery – along the street we found a branch of Rome's famous Castroni gourmet food stores. Because we had to carry our purchases on foot up the hill to the house, it meant one or more visits every day ...

Our house, on the edge of the Villa Borghese, had several rooftop gardens with great views of the city all the way across to the Duomo of St. Peter's. One night, stocked up with pounds of clams from the *Mercato Rionale*, we cooked them with plenty of garlic, chilies and linguine, and settled down with our friends to an outdoor dining experience at the sumptuous marble table on one of the rooftop terraces. We really installed ourselves, with lots of candles, big bowls, and an ample supply of Chianti, congratulating ourselves on our fabulous location. I became aware of a child's face peering at us over a neighboring wall. Soon there was a whole row of faces, young and old. We didn't discover until the next morning that we'd been trespassing. We'd actually been sitting on the neighbors' private terrace. To their credit, they let us have our meal without saying a word.

Rome is always surprising. One evening we had dinner on the pavement at Marcello Restaurant in Via Aurora near Via Veneto. Suddenly, round the corner of Via Ludovisi swept a motorcade of police cars, blue lights spinning. Uniformed men sprang from the cars. A large black limousine glided up, doors flew open, and two sheepish men stepped out and were ushered quickly inside while the security forces stared down the dumbstruck diners. Our waiter was agog and told us it was "important" men traveling "incognito." For the next couple of hours burly men in identical blue suits, who were obviously bodyguards, ate dinner in shifts, whispering on cellular phones. Our flustered waiter took our order for a plate of mixed antipasti to share, and returned after a lengthy delay with four laden dishes of beans, baby artichokes and various salads. A splendid meal, if bearing no resemblance to what we thought we had asked for.

Another great find was Gusto, Rome's foodie mecca in the Piazza Augusto. As well as offering an impressive array of top-brand kitchen equipment, Gusto's restaurants serve down-to-earth food with fabulous, clearly defined flavors. It's trendy and traditional at the same time, and Romans and tourists flock there. For me, Gusto held a surprise. Some years earlier I'd finished my book *Ingredients*, and I hadn't even known there was an Italian translation until I found it on display there. Susanna, the manager, and her wine specialist colleague were so enthused when they found out I had written it. It was a great way to make new friends. And greet an old one.

Linguine with lentils and pancetta
Linguine con lenticchie e pancetta

Lentilles vertes de Puy, *the much admired small, slate-colored lentils from France, are similar to* Castelluccio *lentils from Umbria. Both varieties are quite expensive but worth every cent. Ordinary green or brown supermarket lentils may also be used. Follow this with a green salad.*

1 cup Puy lentils (French green lentils)
3 tablespoons extra virgin olive oil
¼ pound pancetta, cut into thin slivers
2 stalks celery, cut into pea-sized cubes
4 large cloves garlic, chopped
2 teaspoons chopped rosemary leaves
1-2 fresh hot red chilies, sliced, seeds removed, if you like
½ cup dry white wine
¾ pound dried long pasta, such as linguine or pappardelle
good handful fresh-leaf parsley, leaves coarsely chopped

Place the lentils in a saucepan and cover with about 2-inch water. Add salt and cover the pan. Set over low heat and cook until the water comes to a boil. Set the lid on an angle and cook over very low heat until the lentils are tender, about 30 minutes. Remove from the heat and set the lentils aside in their liquid.

Combine the oil and pancetta in a large, deep frying pan and cook over moderate heat until the pancetta is crisp and golden, about 5 minutes. Remove the pancetta with a slotted spoon to a plate lined with paper towels and set aside.

Add the celery to the pan and cook until it begins to soften, about 5 minutes. Add the garlic, rosemary and chilies and cook until fragrant, about 2 minutes. Drain the lentils and add to the celery mixture with the wine and cook until the wine has reduced by half. Check seasoning.

Meanwhile, cook the pasta in plenty of salted, boiling water until al dente. Drain, reserving a small measuring cup of the cooking water. Add the pasta to the lentil mixture and toss over heat for 1 minute. Remove from the heat and toss in the parsley and the reserved pancetta. Serve in deep, heated plates.

Serves 4

Tagliatelle with clams
Tagliatelle alle vongole in bianco

We are very particular about where we buy our clams, a regular weekend lunch in our house. There are now several fishmongers at our local fish markets which keep clams "live" in water. These don't have any grit, which is more than I can say about the clams from the Mercato Rionale (neighborhood market) in Rome.

small handful flat-leaf parsley, with stalks
¼ cup extra virgin olive oil
8 large cloves garlic, chopped
2-4 hot red chilies, split, but left attached at the stem, seeds removed if you like
2 pounds clams (vongole)
¾ pound long dried pasta, such as linguine or tagliatelle
lemon wedges, to serve

Separate the parsley leaves from the stalks. Chop the tender parsley stalks finely and discard the tough stalks. Chop the leaves coarsely and set aside.

Combine the chopped parsley stalks with olive oil, garlic and chilies in a large sauté pan, and cook over moderate heat until fragrant but before the garlic starts to color, about 3 minutes. Add the clams and cook over medium high heat, shaking the pan frequently – you don't have to cover the pan – until all the clams have opened. This should take about 5 minutes. Discard any clams that have not opened.

Meanwhile cook the pasta in plenty of salted boiling water until al dente. Drain the pasta, reserving a small measuring cup of the cooking water. Add the pasta to the sauté pan containing the opened clams. Add the chopped parsley leaves and toss well for 1-2 minutes over moderate heat, adding a little of the cooking water to moisten, if necessary. Turn onto a heated dish and serve immediately, with the clams in their shells, and with the lemon wedges.

Serves 4

Homemade tomato sauce
Salsa di pomodoro casareccia

If good, fresh tomatoes are not on hand or are very expensive (in winter, for example), I'm more than happy to use Italian canned tomatoes in my cooking. You can buy tomato sauces with flavorings added but I've found these disappointing and wouldn't bother with them. This homemade sauce has a lovely, fresh flavor and can be used as is, or diluted with water, stock or wine for a thinner consistency.

3 tablespoons extra virgin olive oil
1 red onion, cut into ¼-inch cubes
4 large cloves garlic, chopped
1½ tablespoons chopped fresh rosemary
1 celery stalk, cut into pea-sized cubes
two 14-ounce cans Italian diced tomatoes

Combine the oil and onion in a large pot and cook over moderate heat until the onion starts to brown, about 10 minutes, stirring frequently. Add the garlic, rosemary and celery and cook another 5-8 minutes, or until the celery is soft.

Stir in the tomatoes and bring to a boil, stirring frequently. Lower the heat to a simmer, set the lid at an angle, and cook until the sauce is thick, about 30 minutes. Season with salt and pepper. This sauce will keep in the refrigerator for up to 1 week, or in the freezer up to 6 months.

Makes 4 cups

Penne with sausage, pancetta and eggs
Penne con salsicce e uova

A close cousin to the recipe on page 30, this version is rather more filling and gutsy, with plenty of sausage. Lemon juice added to the egg mixture lightens the flavor. Definitely not a starter, but a robust main course – all it needs is a green salad to follow.

4 eggs
freshly squeezed juice plus zest of 1 lemon
¾ cup freshly grated parmesan or Pecorino Romano cheese
1½ tablespoons extra virgin olive oil
¼ pound lean pancetta, finely chopped
1 pound homemade sausage (see page 240) or 4 plain Italian sausages, about 1 pound, skins removed, crumbled
¾ pound dried short pasta, such as penne or casareccia
good handful flat-leaf parsley leaves, coarsely chopped

Combine the eggs, lemon juice and zest, and parmesan in a bowl and beat with a fork until smooth. Season with plenty of black pepper and set aside.

Combine the oil and pancetta in a large sauté pan, which can later accommodate the pasta as well, and cook over moderate heat until the pancetta colors, about 3-4 minutes. Remove the pancetta with a slotted spoon and set aside. Add the sausage to the pan and sauté until it colors, about 5 minutes. Return the pancetta to the pan and keep warm.

Meanwhile, cook the pasta in salted, boiling water until nearly al dente. Drain and reserve a small measuring cup of the cooking water. Add the pasta to the sausage mixture, together with some of the reserved pasta cooking water and cook over high heat for 2 minutes.

Remove the pan from the heat and immediately stir in the egg mixture and the parsley. The heat of the sausage will cook the eggs. Transfer to a heated bowl and serve in deep, heated plates.

Serves 4

Spaghetti with eggs and pancetta
Spaghetti alla carbonara

One of Rome's favorites, this classic pasta is a great stand-by after a late night out, in much the same way french onion soup is in Paris. Hot pasta is tossed with an aromatic mixture of oil, garlic, chili and pancetta, immediately followed by eggs beaten with parmesan cheese. The heat of the pasta "cooks" the eggs, transforming them into a creamy sauce, making the addition of cream superfluous. Too often, outside Rome, cream is added.

2 large, very fresh eggs
⅔ cup freshly grated parmesan cheese
⅓ cup extra virgin olive oil
2 large cloves garlic, finely chopped
2-4 fresh red chilies, split and seeds removed, if you like
¼ pound straight pancetta, chopped
1 pound dried spaghetti

Combine the eggs and parmesan in a small bowl, whisk until smooth and set aside. Combine the oil, garlic, chilies and pancetta in a small frying pan and cook over low heat until the pancetta has released most of its fat, making sure the garlic doesn't burn; it has to stay a very pale straw color. Regulate the heat so the pancetta and pasta will be cooked at the same time. If the garlic is in danger of burning, remove the pan from the heat and reheat briefly when pasta is cooked.

Meanwhile cook the spaghetti in plenty of salted boiling water until al dente. Drain, reserving a small measuring cup of the cooking water. Turn the pasta into a heated bowl. Immediately remove the chilies from the frying pan and pour the hot contents of the pan over the pasta, then without delay the eggs and cheese, together with some of the reserved pasta cooking water. Toss well and serve immediately. At the table grind copious amounts of black pepper over the pasta.

Serves 4-6

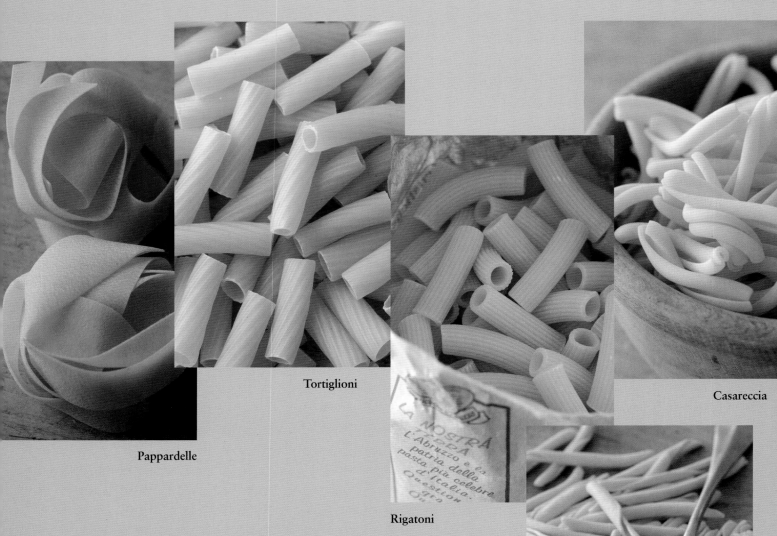

Tortiglioni

Casareccia

Pappardelle

Rigatoni

Fusilli

Cavatelli

Pasta

Penne

Ditalini

Orecchiette

Bucatini, Spaghetti, Linguine

TO COOK PASTA

Bring a large pot of water to a boil. Add salt and, when the water boils furiously, add the pasta. Do not add oil – this only makes the pasta slippery and unable to hold a sauce. Provided you cook the pasta in plenty of water, it will not stick. Stir the pasta from time to time. Take a note of the cooking time on the package and start testing the pasta 2 minutes before the time is up. The only way to test if the pasta is "al dente" – still left with a little bite – is to taste a strand or piece.

When cooked, drain and reserve a small measuring cup of the cooking water. Use this water to thin out the sauce, and bring the cup to the table as well. You'll find by the time second helpings are required, the pasta left in the bowl will have become dry and have absorbed most of the liquid. Stir in some of the reserved cooking water and your pasta will be as new. Remember, this cooking water is not "just water." It contains all the excess starches of the pasta, so it's not merely liquid, it actually has substance.

Pasta

Penne with tomato and meat sauce
Penne al sugo di braciola

Naples is famous for its tomato sauces, but this one is considered to be more of a meat sauce. To set the record straight, it is really two wonderful dishes in one. The rolled up meat (braciola – lit. chop or slice – or vrasciola in Calabrian dialect) flavors the tomato sauce as it cooks.

Long, slow cooking permeates the sauce with hearty meat flavors, and you'll end up with a pasta sauce of unbelievable depth of flavor.

All sorts of meat may be used, and a frequent variation adds a few pork sausages about half an hour before the sauce is cooked, but the meats are always removed, and never served with pasta.

Serve the sauce alone with pasta (penne is traditional), then the meat can be served with a little of the sauce, either on the same night or the next day. This is typical of Naples and the surrounding Campania region.

1 pound round steak in one piece

Meat filling paste
2 large cloves garlic, peeled
handful flat-leaf parsley
¼ cup freshly grated parmesan cheese, plus extra, to serve
1½ tablespoons unsalted butter, at room temperature

Sauce
2 medium red onions, peeled and coarsely chopped
¼ pound pancetta, coarsely copped
1 stalk celery, coarsely chopped
2 large cloves garlic, peeled
large handful flat-leaf parsley
1½ tablespoons unsalted butter
¼ cup extra virgin olive oil
3 tablespoons red wine vinegar
two 14-ounce cans Italian tomatoes, with juice
1 cup degreased chicken or veal stock or broth (see page 223), more if needed

Pasta
2 pounds penne or other short dried pasta, such as casareccia
freshly grated parmesan cheese, to serve

(Continued next page)

Penne with tomato and meat sauce

(Continued from previous page)

Ask the butcher to beat the beef until it is an even thickness and thin enough to roll around a filling. Combine the garlic, parsley, parmesan and butter in a processor and pulse until you have a coarse paste. Season with salt and pepper and spread all over the beef. Roll up the beef and tie securely with kitchen string. Set aside.

To make the sauce, combine the onions, pancetta, celery, garlic and parsley in a processor and pulse until finely chopped. Combine the butter and oil in a large, heavy-based pot and heat over moderate heat until the butter foam starts to subside. Add the meat and brown on all sides, about 10 minutes, then add the vinegar and cook 1 minute. Add the chopped vegetable mixture and cook another 5 minutes, turning the meat from time to time. Season with salt and pepper, then add the tomatoes. Bring to a simmer, breaking the tomatoes up coarsely with a wooden spoon.

Cover the pot securely and simmer over low heat for 1 hour, turning the meat twice. Add the stock and simmer another 1 hour, adding more stock if necessary. The sauce should become very thick and rich. Transfer the meat to a heated serving dish and cover loosely with foil. The meat is now ready to be served. Remove the strings, slice and pour a little of the sauce over the slices. Check the sauce for seasoning and cook a few more minutes with the lid removed, to thicken, if necessary. If too thick, add a little more stock.

Meanwhile, cook the pasta in a large pot of salted, boiling water until al dente. Drain, reserving a small measuring cup of the cooking water. Add the pasta to the meat sauce and cook over moderate heat for 2 minutes, adding a little of the cooking water to moisten, if necessary. Serve in deep, heated plates, with parmesan.

Serves 6-8

Pancetta

*Pancetta is made from the belly of the pig (*pancia – lit. belly*), similar to bacon. The pork is rubbed with salt and spices, then cured for a few weeks. There are several varieties of pancetta available:*

• Straight pancetta (*pancetta stesa*), shown. The rind and a good layer of fat are still attached. I prefer this kind of pancetta for most of my cooking and buy it in fairly large pieces at the deli counter. It keeps well in the refrigerator, and can also be frozen. Available plain or with chili.

• Rolled pancetta (*pancetta arrotolata*). The rind and some of the fat are removed, then the meat is tightly rolled into a thick sausage shape. Available plain or with chili.

If pancetta is not available, bacon and speck can be substituted in most cases, with reasonable results.

BATTUTO
Italian dishes often start off with a finely chopped mixture of garlic, herbs – such as rosemary, thyme and parsley – and vegetables – such as onion, carrots and celery. Sometimes a little pancetta, prosciutto or speck is added, as well.

SOFFRITO
Once the *battuto* is in the pan, and you're actually cooking it, it becomes a *soffrito*. The mixture is gently sautéed in oil, flavoring the dish from the very start. Even the blandest ingredients become impregnated with the savory flavors of the *battuto*, making them instantly more interesting and exciting and giving that unmistakably Italian taste.

Orecchiette with broccoli raab and chickpeas
Orecchiette con broccoli raab e ceci

*Broccoli raab is related to the turnip. It is a favorite bitter green in Apulia
(the "heel of the boot"), and is available in the cooler months. With a peppery,
mustardy flavor, this green is eminently suitable for pasta sauces and it's
usually cooked with plenty of garlic. You can also try this recipe
with chicory. Orecchiette (little ears), the most popular pasta in Apulia, are
the perfect shape to catch the chickpeas in their hollows.*

1 cup dried chickpeas, soaked overnight
sprig of sage
2 large cloves garlic, bruised with the flat side of a cook's knife, plus 4 large cloves garlic, chopped
2 teaspoons extra virgin olive oil, plus 3 tablespoons extra
5 ounces straight pancetta, thinly sliced
1 large bunch broccoli raab, tough stems removed, cut across into ½-inch strips
¾ pound orecchiette or other short dried pasta, such as penne

Cook the chickpeas with the addition of salt, sage, 2 bruised cloves garlic and 2 teaspoons oil
(see page 108). Remove from the heat and reserve in their liquid.

Combine 3 tablespoons oil and the pancetta in a large sauté pan and cook over moderate heat
until the pancetta is golden brown and crisp, about 8 minutes, stirring frequently. Remove
from the pan and set aside to drain on paper towels.

Add 4 chopped cloves garlic to the pan and cook until fragrant, about 2 minutes, then stir in
the broccoli raab. If the pan is not large enough to add all the broccoli raab at once, stir in
a few handfuls first and cook until wilted, then stir in the remaining broccoli raab and sauté
until all the broccoli raab has wilted.

Drain the chickpeas in a colander set over a bowl and add the chickpeas to the broccoli raab.
Measure 1 cup of the cooking liquid and stir into the broccoli raab and chickpea mixture.
Cook another 10-15 minutes, then season with salt and pepper.

Meanwhile, cook the pasta in plenty of salted, boiling water until al dente. Drain, reserving
a small measuring cup of the cooking water. Add the pasta to the broccoli raab mixture
and toss over high heat for 1 minute more, adding a little of the cooking water to moisten, if
necessary. Transfer to a serving dish and sprinkle with the reserved pancetta.
Serve immediately.

Serves 4

Fiocchi d'amore with celery and beans
Fiocchi d'amore con sedano e fagioli

Comforting and fresh simultaneously, this is a combination of al dente pasta, perfectly cooked beans, crunchy celery and crisp, salty pancetta. In frugal Tuscany and neighboring austere Umbria, celery rules!

This simple pasta and beans dish is fabulous even without the meat essence, but if you have a few tablespoons available, try it and taste the difference.

2 cups cooked cranberry beans (also known as borlotti beans, see page 108)
¼ pound pancetta, thinly sliced
3 tablespoons extra virgin olive oil
4 stalks celery with leaves
4 large cloves garlic, chopped
¾ pound short dried pasta, such as fiocchi d'amore (lovers' knots), cavatelli or penne
3 tablespoons meat essence (see page 220), optional but highly recommended

Pulse half of the cranberry beans in a processor until chopped, but not smooth. Set both the chopped and whole beans aside.

Combine the pancetta and oil in a large, deep sauté pan and cook over moderate heat until pancetta is golden and crisp, about 8 minutes. Remove with a slotted spoon to drain on a plate lined with a paper towel.

Cut the celery stalks into pea-sized cubes. Chop the leaves and reserve. Add the celery cubes to the pan and cook until crisp-tender, about 5 minutes. Add the garlic and cook 1 minute more. Stir in both the chopped and whole beans, heat through gently and keep warm.

Meanwhile, cook the pasta in plenty of salted, boiling water until al dente. Drain, reserving a small measuring cup of the cooking water, and add the pasta to the sauté pan. Stir in the meat essence, the reserved chopped celery leaves, and enough of the cooking water to moisten and stir over moderate heat for another 2 minutes. Serve immediately in deep, heated plates, scattered with the reserved pancetta.

Serves 4

Pappardelle with bean ragù
Pappardelle con ragù di fagioli

Pappardelle, pasta ribbons about ¾-inch wide, are most suitable for robust sauces. One famous example is pappardelle with hare sauce (pappardelle con la lepre).

The presence of speck (a fatty cut of salt-cured bacon, also known as lardo *in Italy and* tocino *in Spain) points clearly to the cooking of the northern Italian provinces, such as Venezia Tridentina and the Valle d'Aosta. Here the food is much influenced by Austrian and German cuisines and you'll also frequently find other hearty ingredients, such as potatoes and sauerkraut, to sustain people who are used to living and working in harsh weather.*

2 pounds fresh cranberry beans, shelled, or 2 cups dried cranberry beans, soaked overnight (see page 108)
½ red onion, chopped
¼ pound fatty speck, cut into pea-sized cubes
5 ounces prosciutto in one piece, cut into bite-sized cubes
4 large roma tomatoes, peeled, seeded and coarsely chopped
¾ pound dried pappardelle or other flat long pasta, such as linguine
½ cup chopped flat-leaf parsley

Cook the beans (see page 108) and set aside in their liquid.

Combine the onion and speck in a large pan and cook over moderately low heat until the onions are golden and the speck fat starts to run, about 10 minutes. Stir in the prosciutto and cook 5 minutes, stirring frequently.

Drain the beans, reserving the liquid, and add the beans to the pan, together with the tomatoes and enough of the bean cooking liquid to just cover the beans. Season with salt and simmer over low heat until the beans are very tender, but not falling apart, about 30-40 minutes. Check seasoning and keep warm.

Meanwhile cook the pasta in plenty of salted, boiling water until al dente and drain, reserving a small measuring cup of the cooking water. Toss the pasta and the parsley into the bean sauce, adding a little of the cooking water to moisten, if necessary. Serve in deep, heated plates.

Serves 4

Linguine with calamari, garlic and lemon
Linguine con calamari, aglio e limone

Another regular weekend lunch, and not the first time it's appeared in one of my books. Sergio, a keen young chef in a small trattoria in Toarmina in Sicily, taught me his grandmother's recipe, and it's become one of our favorites; it's so delicious I think you should try it. Make sure you use a juicy lemon, as the lemon juice is a very important component. I find this pasta works best for two, but you can double it if your pan is big enough. If I had to choose a last meal before the gallows, this would have to be it.

good handful flat-leaf parsley, with stalks
4 cloves garlic, chopped
1-2 hot red chilies, sliced, seeds removed, if you like
3 tablespoons extra virgin olive oil
¾ pound calamari, cleaned, bodies sliced into rings, wings scored with a sharp
  knife, tentacles left whole (see page 46)
½ pound long dried pasta, such as linguine or spaghetti
freshly squeezed juice of 1 lemon

Remove the leaves from the parsley, chop coarsely and set aside. Chop the tender parts of the stalks and discard the tough stalks.

Combine the chopped parsley stalks in a deep pan with the garlic, chilies and oil, and cook over very low heat until fragrant.

Meanwhile, cook the pasta in salted, boiling water until al dente. Drain, reserving a measuring cup of the cooking water.

Set the pan with the garlic over high heat and, when hot, add all of the calamari. Season lightly with salt and sauté until opaque, about 1 minute. Add ½ cup of the reserved pasta cooking water and the lemon juice and cook until the liquid comes to a boil, about 1 minute.

Add the drained pasta to the calamari and toss over heat for 2 minutes. Add the reserved chopped parsley leaves, toss again, adding more of the reserved pasta cooking water, if necessary. Transfer to a heated bowl and serve in deep, heated plates, or at room temperature.

Serves 2

Calamari and squid

TO BUY

Buy sweet-smelling calamari with a body length of 4-8 inches, with tentacles intact.
All parts of calamari, except for the "beak" and the "quill", are edible.

TO PREPARE

Pull out the head and tentacles.

Cut off the head just below the eyes.

Holding the tentacles in your hand, turn them upside down *and* push up the little beak in the center (this part is very hard and indigestible). Discard the beak. Leave the tentacles whole or cut in half through the middle, if large. There are 10 tentacles, with two of these appreciably longer than the others. Cut in between the two long tentacles to halve them. Set aside.

Remove the wings from the outside of the body and rub off the skin, if you like (this is a purely cosmetic choice).

Remove and discard the clear plastic-looking quill from inside the body, along with any white roe or foreign material (tiny fish etc).

Rinse out the inside and use as indicated in individual recipes.

The skin may be removed or left on, as you like. I lean towards the rustic look of the purply, mottled skin left on.

TO COOK

For tender calamari, cook either very quickly over intense heat, about 1 minute, or very slowly, over very low heat, about 45-60 minutes. Anything in between will lead to a tough result.

An Italian salad dressing consists just of salt, oil and vinegar.
Use the old saying as a guide: "Judicious with the salt, a spendthrift with
the oil, a miser with the vinegar." Always whisk the salt in the vinegar first to
dissolve it, and then you can start adding the oil.

Casareccia with eggplant in the oven
Casareccia con melanzane al forno

Smoked mozzarella cheese has an incomparable flavor that combines harmoniously with eggplant, and it's well worth the effort to find it. Many deli counters, especially Italian ones, stock it but if you can't find it, substitute with plain mozzarella or a mild provolone.

2 medium eggplants, cut into ¾-inch cubes
1½ tablespoons salt
1 pound short dried pasta, such as casareccia or tortiglioni
¼ cup extra virgin olive oil, plus 1½ tablespoons extra, for the pasta, plus 1½ tablespoons
  extra, for the breadcrumb topping
3 cups homemade tomato sauce (see page 26)
handful coarsely torn basil leaves
1 pound smoked mozzarella cheese, cut into pea-sized cubes
⅔ cup freshly grated parmesan cheese
1 cup fluffy, fresh breadcrumbs (see page 273)

Preheat oven to 375°F. Place the eggplant in a colander, add the salt and toss with your hands. Let stand 30 minutes.

Cook the pasta in plenty of salted, boiling water until al dente. Drain, reserving a measuring cup of the cooking water. Set pasta aside in a large bowl and stir in 1½ tablespoons oil to prevent it from sticking.

Heat ¼ cup oil in a frying pan or wok and fry the eggplant over high heat until brown, without crowding the pan. If the pan is not large enough, do this in 2 batches. Remove with a slotted spoon and add to the pasta in the bowl.

Add the tomato sauce to the pasta and eggplant, stir in the basil, mozzarella and half the parmesan. Add about ½ cup of the pasta cooking water to moisten and season with salt and pepper. Spoon into a large baking dish.

Mix the breadcrumbs in a bowl with the remaining parmesan and the extra tablespoon oil and mix well. Scatter over the dish, "tent" with foil and bake for 40 minutes. Remove the foil and turn the heat up to 400°F and bake another 10 minutes or until the topping is crisp and browning and the pasta mixture is bubbling.

Serves 6

Tortiglioni and mushrooms in the oven
Tortiglioni con funghi al forno

The flavor here doesn't come solely from the dried porcini themselves; their soaking liquid is also used to make a beautiful, velvety sauce, augmented with a small amount of sour cream. Followed with a green salad, it's perfect for an autumn lunch or supper. A class act and suitable for vegetarians.

¾ cup dried porcini mushrooms
3 tablespoons unsalted butter, plus 1 tablespoon extra
1½ tablespoons all-purpose flour
¾ cup sour cream
2 teaspoons chopped fresh thyme leaves
1 small red onion, chopped
1 pound fresh mushrooms of your choice, thickly sliced
¾ pound short dried pasta, such as tortiglioni or penne
½ cup freshly grated Pecorino Romano or parmesan cheese

Preheat oven to 375°F.

Place the dried porcini in a bowl and cover with 2 cups boiling water. Let stand for 20 minutes, or until needed. Drain the porcini, reserving the soaking water. Check the porcini for grit and set aside. Strain the mushroom soaking water through a damp paper towel lining a sieve. Measure the water in a jug, you should have 2 cups. If you don't, supplement with tap water.

Melt 3 tablespoons butter in a pan over moderate heat. Stir in the flour and stir for 3 minutes. Off the heat, add the mushroom liquid all at once. Return to the heat and cook until the mixture comes to a boil and thickens, stirring constantly. Stir in the sour cream and thyme and simmer gently for 10 minutes, stirring from time to time. Check seasoning.

Meanwhile, melt the extra butter in a frying pan set over moderate heat. Add the onion and cook until soft, about 5 minutes, stirring frequently. Add the fresh mushrooms and cook until tender, about 5 minutes. Stir in the mushroom sauce and the reserved porcini, and season with salt and pepper. Transfer the mixture to a large bowl.

Meanwhile, cook the pasta in plenty of salted, boiling water until nearly al dente. Drain, reserving a small measuring cup of the cooking water. Stir the pasta into the mushroom mixture, adding a little of the cooking water to moisten, if necessary. Transfer the mixture to a lightly oiled baking dish and sprinkle with the cheese. Bake for 30 minutes, or until the mixture is bubbly and browned on top. Let stand 5 minutes before serving.

Serves 4

Penne with meatballs in the oven
Penne con polpette al forno

A baked pasta that will please the whole family. You can make it well ahead of time.

3 tablespoons extra virgin olive oil
2 large cloves garlic, finely chopped
¼ pound pancetta or bacon, coarsely chopped
two 14-ounce cans Italian tomatoes, chopped with juice
⅓ cup chopped flat-leaf parsley
1 pound short dried pasta, such as penne or casareccia
½ pound fresh mozzarella cheese, such as bocconcini (about 4), cut into small cubes
1 cup ricotta
⅓ cup freshly grated parmesan cheese, plus 3 tablespoons extra, for the top

Meatballs
1 thick slice Italian-type bread, crusts removed
⅓ cup milk
1 pound minced veal
2 cloves garlic, finely chopped
1 large egg, lightly beaten
¼ cup freshly grated parmesan cheese
3 tablespoons chopped flat-leaf parsley
3 tablespoons extra virgin olive oil

Preheat oven to 400°F.

Make the meatballs first: soak the bread in the milk until the milk has been absorbed. Squeeze the bread dry, crumble into a bowl, together with the veal, garlic, egg, parmesan and parsley. Mix well and season with salt and pepper. Roll into small balls with wet hands. Heat a frying pan over high heat, add oil and when hot but not smoking, add the balls and brown them on all sides, shaking the pan regularly, so they brown evenly. Set aside.

Combine the oil, garlic and pancetta in a frying pan and cook over moderately low heat until the pancetta fat runs, about 5 minutes. Add tomatoes and parsley, bring to a boil, then simmer over moderate heat until the sauce thickens, about 20 minutes. Check seasoning.

Cook the penne in plenty of boiling, salted water until nearly al dente. Drain, reserving a small measuring cup of the cooking water. Combine the pasta in a large bowl with the tomato sauce, the meatballs, bocconcini, ricotta and ⅓ cup of the parmesan. Add enough of the cooking liquid to keep moist.

Transfer to a baking dish, sprinkle with the remaining 3 tablespoons parmesan and bake for 20 minutes until the top is golden with charred peaks and the cheeses are bubbly. Serve hot.

Serves 6-8

Rigatoni with cabbage and fontina in the oven
Rigatoni con verza e fontina al forno

Of all the pasta recipes I've given in my cooking classes over the years, this is one of the most popular, and no wonder! It's very much a product of the Val d'Aosta region, a cold alpine area, where the famous fontina cheese is made and often cooked in conjunction with potatoes and other starches. In Lombardy, buckwheat pasta is often used. Buckwheat grows in Valtellina, which is east of Milan and the home of splendid Valtellina wines. Savoy cabbage is yet another much used local product. Try to find real Italian fontina in a specialty cheese shop – other countries also make fontina, but the flavor is disappointingly nondescript and simply doesn't measure up!

¼ cup extra virgin olive oil
1 small onion, finely chopped
2 cloves garlic, finely chopped
6 sage leaves
10 ounces short dried pasta, such as rigatoni or penne
1 large floury potato, such as Yukon gold or russet, peeled and cut into ½-inch cubes
5 cups savoy cabbage, cut into ½-inch strips
⅔ cup fontina or other good melting cheese, such as gruyere or raclette, thinly sliced
¾ cup freshly grated parmesan cheese

Preheat oven to 350°F.

Combine the oil and onion in a small frying pan and cook over moderately low heat until onion is soft, about 5 minutes. Add the garlic and sage and stir 1 minute more. Set aside.

Cook the pasta in a large pot of salted, boiling water until nearly tender. Drain the pasta, catching the water in another pot. Rinse the pasta. Return the water in the new pot to a boil, add potatoes and cook until just tender, about 7 minutes.

Return pasta to the pot with the potatoes and add cabbage. Stir until cabbage wilts, about 1 minute. Drain the pasta, potato and cabbage, reserving a small jug of the cooking liquid. Stir the onion mixture into the pasta mixture.

Spoon half of the pasta into a lightly oiled baking dish, spoon over half the cheeses and season. Top with the remaining pasta and cheeses and season. Pour about ⅓ cup of the reserved cooking liquid down the sides. Cover with foil and bake for 20-30 minutes to melt the cheese. Flash briefly under a hot broiler to brown the top and serve immediately.

Serves 4

Butternut gnocchi with sage
Gnocchi di zucca alla salvia

Perfect for a starter to a winter meal, these gnocchi are extremely simple to make. You can even make them ahead of time and reheat them in the oven, but don't refrigerate them.

1 pound winter squash with skin on, preferably butternut, seeds removed
2 eggs
grated zest of 1 lemon
pinch of sugar
2 teaspoons Marsala or brandy
freshly grated nutmeg
1⅓ cup all-purpose flour, or more if necessary
4 tablespoons unsalted butter, at room temperature
handful sage leaves

Cut the butternut squash into large pieces, and bake on a lightly oiled baking sheet in a 375°F oven for 30 minutes, or until easily pierced with a skewer. Remove the skin and press the butternut squash through a potato ricer, a mouli, or grate in a processor. Don't process to a puree, as this will make it too smooth.

Combine the squash, eggs, lemon zest, sugar, and marsala in a bowl and season with salt, pepper and nutmeg. Beat until well combined, then stir in the flour and mix thoroughly until well blended, and the mixture starts to come away from the sides of the bowl. Stir in 1-3 tablespoons extra flour, if necessary.

Make little dumplings, using two teaspoons – scoop up a teaspoon full, and use the other spoon to scrape off – and drop into a large pan of salted, simmering water. Do this in batches of about six at a time. Stir so they don't stick to the bottom, and cook 2 minutes, or until they float to the surface. Remove with a slotted spoon, drain briefly on paper towels and place in a generously buttered, heated dish.

Melt the butter in a small pan, add the sage leaves and wilt for a minute. Serve the gnocchi immediately, tossed in the sage butter, or reheat in a 350°F oven for 10 minutes.

Serves 6

Semolina gnocchi in the oven
Gnocchi alla romana

The orginal Gnocchi alla romana, *made with semolina and milk, are one of the cornerstones of true Roman cooking. Make sure you don't cut short on the initial 15 minutes of cooking the semolina, or the gnocchi may fall apart later. They can be made in advance and refrigerated. Pop the whole dish in the oven when ready to serve. The goat's cheese makes a delicious, tangy addition. Alternatively, you can use Italian fontina.*

4 cups milk
1 teaspoon salt
1⅓ cup coarse semolina
1½ tablespoons unsalted butter, at room temperature, plus 1½ tablespoons extra
¾ cup freshly grated parmesan cheese, plus 3 tablespoons, for the top
2 egg yolks
⅓ cup chicken stock or broth (see page 223)
⅓ cup soft goat's cheese, such as chevre, crumbled

Bring the milk and salt to a simmer in a large pot, add the semolina and whisk until there are no lumps. Simmer for 15 minutes, stirring frequently, then remove from the heat. Beat in 1½ tablespoons butter and ¾ cup parmesan, and season with salt. Stir in the egg yolks.

Pour the mixture on to a wet baking sheet and spread with a wet spatula to a ¼-inch thickness. Refrigerate for 1 hour or overnight.

Preheat the oven to 375°F.

Use a 2-inch cutter or a glass to cut out discs. Overlap the discs in a shallow greased baking dish, or place flat on a baking sheet, without overlapping.

Combine the extra butter with the chicken stock in a small pan and bring to a simmer. Pour over the gnocchi, season with salt and pepper and sprinkle with the remaining 3 tablespoons parmesan. Bake 40 minutes for the overlapping gnocchi, or until the top is golden and crisp at the edges. For the gnocchi on the baking sheet without overlapping, bake about 25 minutes, or until the edges are browned and crisp. Scatter the goat's cheese over the gnocchi and bake another 5 minutes, just to soften the cheese. Serve hot.

Serves 6

Bechamel sauce
Salsa balsamella, besciamella

Closely related to French béchamel, this sauce is used extensively in the Italian kitchen, in pasta dishes (lasagna), crepes and other savory preparations.

7 tablespoons unsalted butter
¾ cup all-purpose flour
3¼ cups milk, plus more, if necessary
pinch freshly grated nutmeg

Melt the butter in a saucepan over moderately low heat, stir in the flour and cook 3 minutes, stirring constantly and without the flour browning. Remove from the heat and stir in the milk all at once. Return to the heat and stir over moderate heat until the mixture is simmering. Stir in nutmeg and ½ teaspoon salt.

Simmer 5 minutes, or until the sauce is thick and creamy. Season with pepper and set aside to cool. This sauce is best made on the day it's used. To prevent a skin forming, press a piece of buttered parchment paper on top. If you find the sauce too thick, stir in a little extra milk.

Makes generous 3 cups

Rice & Grains

Venetian rice and peas
Risi e bisi

Is it a soup? Is it a risotto? Well, it actually is neither of these. The Venetians claim this "celebration of springtime" dish as their own, although Paduans protest it's theirs as well. Risi e bisi is always served as a starter but often, interestingly, with a fork. Don't cook this ahead of time – the rice will keep on absorbing the stock and it will become a sticky mush.

1½ tablespoons extra virgin olive oil
1 white onion, chopped
3 pounds peas in the pod, shelled
6 cups chicken stock or broth (see page 223), simmering
1½ cups risotto rice, such as arborio, vialone nano or carnaroli
¼ cup chopped flat-leaf parsley
⅓ cup freshly grated parmesan cheese

Combine the oil and onion in a large pan and cook over moderate heat until the onion is soft, about 5 minutes, stirring frequently. Add the peas and a ladleful of stock and simmer 10 minutes, stirring frequently.

Add the remaining stock all at once, bring to a boil, then stir in the rice. Simmer, stirring frequently, until the rice is al dente, about 15-20 minutes. Stir in the parsley and parmesan and season with salt and pepper. Serve immediately in deep, heated plates.

Serves 4

Pancetta, red wine and radicchio risotto
Risotto con pancetta, vino rosso e radicchio

*The rice equivalent of a hearty beef and red wine stew, reserve this risotto for
a chilly night in front of the fire. If you have meat essence, please don't forget to use
it here, it makes this risotto so luxurious and velvety smooth, you'll wish you
could go on eating forever ...*

1½ tablespoons extra virgin olive oil
½ pound pancetta, cut into small pea-sized cubes
1 red onion, chopped
2 cloves garlic, finely chopped
2 cups risotto rice, such as arborio, vialone nano or carnaroli
2 cups dry red wine, such as Chianti
1 large radicchio, quartered and thinly sliced
4 cups chicken, veal or beef stock or broth (see page 223), simmering
cup meat essence (see page 220), optional
¼ cup freshly grated parmesan cheese

Combine the oil and pancetta in a large, heavy-based pan. Sauté over moderate heat until
browning and the fat starts to run, about 8 minutes. Add the onion and cook until soft, about
another 5 minutes. Add the garlic and stir 1 minute more.

Add the rice and stir a few minutes to coat. Add the wine and stir until it has been absorbed,
about 5-8 minutes. Add the radicchio and a ladleful of the simmering stock and stir until
the stock has been absorbed. Continue adding stock in this manner until the rice is al dente,
about 20 minutes. Adjust the heat sources below the stock and risotto so they simmer at
about the same temperature. Season with salt and pepper halfway through cooking. If
the stock runs out before the rice is cooked, continue cooking with simmering water.

When the rice is al dente, remove the pot from the heat, add the meat essence and parmesan,
and stir in vigorously. Check seasoning, cover the pot and let stand 3 minutes before serving
in deep, heated plates.

Serves 4

Risotto with saffron
Risotto alla milanese

The use of saffron in Risotto alla milanese *may be explained by the Spanish occupation of Milan during the second half of the 16th century – in fact, this risotto is probably closely related to Spanish* paella. *Italian cooks of that time would use spices such as saffron with abandon, frequently overdoing it. These days* Risotto alla milanese *is nearly always served as an accompaniment to* Ossobuco *(see page 242), although true Milanese eat it also as a meal on its own.*

¼ teaspoon saffron threads
3 tablespoons extra virgin olive oil
1 onion, chopped
1 clove garlic, finely chopped
2 cups risotto rice, such as arborio, vialone nano or carnaroli
½ cup dry white wine
6 cups veal or chicken stock, or broth (see page 223), simmering
⅔ cup freshly grated parmesan cheese

Place the saffron in a small bowl and cover with 1½ tablespoons hot water. Let stand for 20 minutes, or until needed.

Combine the oil and onion in a large, round, heavy-bottomed pan and stir over moderate heat until onion is soft, about 5 minutes. Add the garlic and stir 1 minute. Add the rice and stir until all the grains are well coated, about 2 minutes.

Add the wine and stir until it has been absorbed. Add a ladleful of the stock and stir until it has been absorbed. Continue adding the stock in this manner until the rice is al dente, about 20 minutes. Halfway through cooking (after about 10 minutes adding stock) add the saffron and its soaking liquid with the next ladle of stock, and season lightly with salt and pepper. Reserve a few tablespoons stock to stir in last. If the stock runs out before the rice is cooked, continue with simmering water.

When the rice is cooked, stir in the reserved tablespoons of the stock and the parmesan. Stir vigorously over the heat, then remove the pan from the heat and cover with a lid. Let stand for 3 minutes, then serve in deep, heated plates.

Serves 6

Mushroom risotto
Risotto con funghi

Dried porcini mushrooms are a great standby. While hard to get when fresh, these dried exotic beauties are readily available, and together with ordinary field mushrooms, pack an almighty punch.

¾ cup dried porcini mushrooms
3 tablespoons extra virgin olive oil, plus 2 tablespoons extra for the mushrooms
1 onion, chopped
2 cups risotto rice, such as arborio, vialone nano or carnaroli
½ cup dry white wine
6 cups chicken, veal or vegetable stock or broth (see page 223), simmering
2-4 large cloves garlic, finely chopped
2 pounds mixed exotic fresh mushrooms, or plain field mushrooms, sliced, halved or left whole, depending on size
⅔ cup freshly grated parmesan cheese
generous handful flat-leaf parsley, chopped

Place the dried porcini in a small bowl and cover with boiling water. Let stand for at least 20 minutes, or until ready to use. Drain the porcini in a sieve lined with damp kitchen paper, set over a bowl to catch the liquid. Check the porcini for grit and chop roughly. Set aside the porcini and the liquid separately.

Combine 2 tablespoons oil and onion in a heavy-based, round-bottomed pan and cook over moderate heat until the onion is soft, about 5 minutes, stirring frequently. Add the rice and stir 2 minutes to coat. Add the wine and stir until it has been absorbed. Start adding the simmering stock, one ladle at a time, and stir until it has been absorbed. Continue adding stock in this manner until the rice is al dente, which should take about 20 minutes. Add the reserved porcini liquid and season with salt and pepper halfway through cooking time. If the stock runs out before the rice is cooked, continue adding simmering water. Reserve a few tablespoons stock to stir in last.

Meanwhile, cook the fresh mushrooms. Combine 3 tablespoons oil and the garlic in a frying pan and cook over low heat until the garlic is fragrant, about 3 minutes, stirring frequently. Add the mushrooms and turn up the heat. Cook for 3-5 minutes, tossing constantly. Stir in the reserved dried porcini and season with salt and pepper.

When the rice is al dente, stir in the mushrooms, parmesan and parsley, and the reserved stock. Stir vigorously, cover the pan and let stand 3 minutes before serving in deep, heated plates.

Serves 4

Greens play an important role in Italy every day – a salad is always served and people are very choosy about quality and freshness. A good shopkeeper is not just a supplier but is valued as someone to ask for advice and even to share recipes with.

Risotto with arugula and taleggio
Risotto con rucola e taleggio

These days arugula seems synonymous with Italian cooking, but it actually originates in Asia. The slightly peppery taste complements rice and cheese beautifully. Don't use baby arugula, you need a sturdier leaf that will wilt without disintegrating completely. Any other bitter green, such as broccoli raab, chicory or even watercress, are good substitutes in this risotto.

3 tablespoons extra virgin olive oil
1 small onion, chopped
2 large cloves garlic, finely chopped
2 cups risotto rice, such as arborio, vialone nano or carnaroli
½ cup dry white wine
6 cups chicken stock or broth (see page 223), simmering
1 bunch arugula, coarsely chopped
½ cup taleggio or fontina cheese, cut into small pieces

Combine the oil and onion in a heavy-based, deep pan and cook over moderate heat until the onion is soft, about 5 minutes, stirring frequently. Add the garlic and stir 1 further minute.

Add the rice and stir for a few minutes, so every grain is coated. Add the wine and stir over moderate heat until it has been absorbed. Add a ladleful of the simmering stock and stir over moderate heat until the stock has been absorbed. Keep adding stock and stirring until it has been absorbed before adding the next ladle. Cook until the rice is al dente, about 20 minutes from the time you start adding the stock. Season with salt and pepper about halfway through cooking time. Reserve a few tablespoons of the stock to stir in at the very last moment. If the stock runs out before the risotto is cooked, continue, adding simmering water.

When the rice is cooked and the last addition of stock has been absorbed, add the reserved stock, the arugula and taleggio, and stir in vigorously. Cover the pan and let stand 3 minutes before serving in deep, heated plates.

Serves 4

Sausage and cranberry bean risotto
Risotto con salsicce e fagioli borlotti

A splendid example of cucina povera: *humble ingredients, nutritious and so delicious!*

1 pound fresh cranberry beans, shelled, or ½ cup dried cranberry beans, soaked overnight or
  quick-soaked (see page 108)
1½ tablespoons extra virgin olive oil
1 onion, chopped
7 ounces homemade sausage (see page 240), or the same quantity Italian sausages without fennel, meat removed
  from the casings and crumbled
2 cups risotto rice, such as arborio, vialone nano or carnaroli
½ cup dry white wine
6 cups chicken or veal stock or broth (see page 223), simmering
½ cup freshly grated parmesan cheese
¼ cup chopped flat-leaf parsley

Simmer the fresh beans in plenty of lightly salted water until tender, about 30-40 minutes.
Reserve in their cooking water and set aside. If using soaked dried beans, drain them and
cover with fresh, lightly salted water. Simmer until tender, about 30-40 minutes, depending on
their age.

Combine the oil and onion in a heavy-based pan and cook over moderate heat until
onion is soft, about 5 minutes, stirring frequently. Stir in the sausage and cook until golden.
Drain the cooked beans and add them to the pan, together with a few tablespoons of their
cooking liquid.

Mash about half of the beans against the sides of the pan and cook 1 minute more, then stir
in the rice. Add ½ cup wine and stir over moderate heat until it has been absorbed. Add a
ladleful of the simmering stock and stir until absorbed. Continue adding stock in this manner
until the rice is al dente, about 20 minutes. Season with salt and pepper after about 10
minutes. Reserve a few tablespoons stock to stir in last.

Add the parmesan, parsley and reserved stock and stir vigorously. Remove from the heat,
cover with a lid and let stand 3 minutes before serving in deep, heated plates.

Serves 4

Mussel risotto
Risotto alle cozze

A Venetian specialty, this should be served all'onda, *on a wave, indicating the dish should be quite liquid and creamy in texture – the opposite of stiff and dry.*

3½ pounds black mussels in the shell
½ cup dry white wine
¼ cup extra virgin olive oil
1 red onion, chopped
4 cloves garlic, finely chopped
2 cups risotto rice, such as arborio, vialone nano or carnaroli
4 cups fish stock or chicken stock or broth (see page 223), simmering
¼ cup chopped flat-leaf parsley

Scrub the mussels if necessary and remove the beards. Combine the mussels in a large pan with the wine and set over high heat. Cover with a lid and cook until the mussels have opened, shaking the pan vigorously from time to time. Remove the mussels with tongs as they open. Discard any mussels that will not open after extra cooking time. Reserve the liquid in the pan. Take the mussels from the shells, reserving any liquid: add this to the mussel cooking liquid in the pan. Sieve this liquid through damp paper towels and add to the simmering stock. Check the seasoning, adding salt and pepper, if necessary. Halve or quarter very large mussels, but leave small ones whole. Set the mussels aside.

Combine the oil and onion in a large, round-bottomed pan and cook over moderate heat until soft, about 5 minutes, stirring frequently. Add the garlic and stir 1 minute more. Add the rice and stir until all the grains are coated and begin to change color, about 2 minutes. Add a ladleful of the simmering stock and stir until the stock has been absorbed. Continue adding stock in this manner until the rice is al dente, about 20 minutes from the first addition. Season the risotto about half-way through the cooking time. If the stock runs out before the rice is al dente, continue with simmering water. Keep a ladleful of stock to stir in last.

When the rice is al dente, stir in the last ladleful of the stock, the reserved mussels and the parsley. Stir for 1-2 minutes to heat the mussels. Cover the pan and remove from the heat. Let stand 3 minutes before serving in deep, heated plates.

Serves 4-6

Rice stuffed tomatoes on potatoes
Pomodori ripieni di riso

You'd almost never find an antipasto *table in an Italian restaurant without rice-stuffed tomatoes, along with the endless list of various sliced meats, such as prosciutto and coppa, frittata, marinated eggplant and mushrooms. The thrifty Italian housewife has gone one step further, and made a complete meal out of these stuffed tomatoes, baking them on thickly sliced potatoes. A delicious and filling meatless meal.*

4 large, ripe tomatoes
4 starchy potatoes, such as Yukon gold, cooked in their skin, peeled, and cut into ¾-inch thick slices
½ cup arborio rice, cooked until al dente and drained
1 large clove garlic, finely chopped
handful mixed flat-leaf parsley and basil, chopped
3 tablespoons extra virgin olive oil

Preheat oven to 375°F.

Cut about ½-inch off the top of the tomatoes and set the "lids" aside. Hollow out the tomatoes over a sieve, and reserve the juices. Lightly salt the inside of the tomatoes, and turn them upside down until needed.

Place the potatoes in an oiled dish in one layer. Mix the cooked rice in a bowl with garlic and herbs, season with salt and pepper, and use to stuff the tomatoes firmly. Pour a teaspoon of the reserved tomato juice over the rice in each tomato, or as much as it will absorb.

Place the filled tomatoes on the potatoes and arrange the lids on top. Drizzle the oil over the potatoes and bake for 30 minutes or until the potatoes are slightly crisp and golden. Serve hot, in deep, heated plates.

Serves 4

Rice salad with sausage, fennel and grapes
Insalata di riso con salsicce, finocchio e uva

In Italy this beautiful salad is often made during the grape harvest. Make sure you buy really flavorful, coarse-textured sausages.

2 cups risotto rice, such as arborio, vialone nano or carnaroli
3 tablespoons freshly squeezed lemon juice
¼ cup extra virgin olive oil
½ fennel bulb, cut into pea-sized cubes
½ small red onion, finely diced
1 large clove garlic, very finely chopped
1 pound best-quality coarse-textured Italian sausages
3 cups seedless grapes
few handfuls lettuce leaves, optional

Cook the rice in lightly salted water until al dente, about 11 minutes. Drain, rinse under cold water and drain again. Stir in the lemon juice, oil, fennel, onion and garlic, and season with salt and pepper.

Prick the sausages all over and grill until cooked through. Allow to cool on paper towels and cut into bite-sized pieces. Add sausages and grapes to rice, check seasoning and let stand a few minutes before serving. Serve on lettuce leaves, if you like.

Serves 4

Rice cake with provolone and sausage
Bomba di riso

A rice cake with a difference – great served hot from the oven, but equally nice when made a day ahead. When served hot, the rice will have formed a golden, crisp crust, leaving the inside soft and runny. When refrigerated overnight, the cheese filling sets firm and the cake may be sliced into wedges. Perfect for a picnic!

1¼ cup risotto rice, such as vialone nano, arborio or carnaroli
2 eggs, lightly beaten
¼ cup freshly grated parmesan cheese
tiny pinch of nutmeg

Provolone and sausage filling
1 teaspoon extra virgin olive oil
5 ounces homemade sausage (see page 240) or store-bought coarse-textured Italian sausage, meat removed
  from casing, and crumbled
¾ cup ricotta cheese
¾ cup provolone cheese, *dolce* (mild) or *piccante* (sharp), cut into ½-inch cubes
¼ cup chopped prosciutto
⅓ cup shelled peas, boiled until bright green and tender

Preheat the oven to 350°F and butter a 8-inch springform cake tin.

Cook the rice in lightly salted water until al dente, about 14 minutes. Drain well and place in a large bowl. Add the eggs and parmesan, and season with salt and pepper, and nutmeg.

Heat the oil in a non-stick sauté pan, add the crumbled sausage meat and sauté until the meat is cooked through and golden, about 8 minutes. Set aside.

In a large bowl, combine the ricotta, provolone, prosciutto, peas and the cooked sausage and mix well. Season with salt and pepper.

Spoon half of the rice mixture into the prepared cake tin, top with the cheese mixture, then finish with the remaining rice, levelling the surface. Bake 40 minutes, or until the top is golden and crisp. Remove from the oven and let stand 10 minutes, then remove the spring form and slide on to a platter. Cut into wedges to serve.

Serves 6-8

Grilled Polenta

The consistency of this polenta is firm, so it doesn't fall apart easily when handled, which is important when grilling. Butter or cheese, such as parmesan, Pecorino or fontina may be stirred in immediately when cooked. If you like to serve soft polenta as an accompaniment, or to layer in lasagne, use the recipe below.

6 cups water
2 teaspoon salt
2 cups cornmeal (polenta)
extra virgin olive oil

Combine the water and salt in a large saucepan and bring to a boil. Reduce heat to a steady simmer and pour the cornmeal in gradually – traditionally through a clenched fist, but I find that a steady stream is just fine – stirring all the while. Cook over low heat, stirring constantly, until the polenta pulls away from the sides of the pan, about 20 minutes. Immediately pour into a lightly oiled, oblong cake tin (or tins) and leave to cool. When cool, turn out and slice with a sharp knife. Brush each side with oil and cook under a hot griller until crusty on both sides. Alternatively cook on a ridged stove-top griller pan, which will give the slices attractive grill marks.

Serves 8-12

Soft Polenta

The consistency of this polenta is light, soft and creamy, great for serving with stews, game and sausages. When cooled and set, this polenta may be sliced to serve as layers in lasagne, in which case don't add the butter, but pour into a large, oiled, oblong cake tin, or two medium ones, and cool until set.

8 cups water
3 tablespoons extra virgin olive oil
3 teaspoon salt
2 cups cornmeal (polenta)
4 tablespoons unsalted butter, cut into cubes

The procedure is the same as for grilled polenta (see above). Add the oil to the water, together with the salt, as soon as it comes to the boil. The moment the polenta is cooked, stir in the butter until melted and well incorporated. Along with the butter, you can stir in freshly grated parmesan, fontina or gruyere cheese. Serve immediately in a heated bowl. Serves 6-8

PRESSURE COOKER POLENTA
The method is identical, but after all the cornmeal has been added, simply cover, bring up the pressure and cook over low heat for 20 minutes. Perfect polenta without stirring!

INSTANT OR 1-MINUTE POLENTA (see page 88)

Polenta lasagna with three cheeses
Lasagna di polenta

The people coming to my classes, both the very experienced cooks and the keen novices, have one thing in common: they like things to be easy. For this reason, I gave them the following recipe, made with 1-minute polenta. Previously I made this ultimate in comfort food with polenta made the "proper" way but I must say the difference in taste is minimal.

Polenta
1 pound pack 1-minute polenta
3 teaspoons salt

Bechamel sauce
4 tablespoons unsalted butter
⅓ cup all-purpose flour
2 cups milk

Lasagna
two 14-ounce cans Italian peeled tomatoes, coarsely chopped in a processor with their juice
⅓ cup blue cheese
⅔ cup freshly grated Pecorino Romano cheese
¼ cup finely chopped fontina, gruyere or raclette cheese

Preheat oven to 375°F.

Make the polenta first: bring 8 cups water to a boil, add the salt, stir until salt has dissolved. Remove from the heat and add the polenta in a steady stream. Stir 1 minute, then pour into an oiled cake tin. Let cool and set, then cut into ½-inch slices and set aside.

Make the bechamel sauce: melt the butter in a pan, stir in the flour and cook gently for a few minutes, stirring frequently. Remove from the heat and pour in all the milk at once. Bring to a simmer, stirring constantly. When the sauce thickens, season with salt and pepper, and simmer gently for 6-8 minutes.

Spread two-thirds of the tomatoes and their juice in a lasagna dish. Make a layer with the polenta slices, cutting to size to make them fit. Crumble the blue cheese over the top and spread with half the bechamel and another layer polenta slices. There may be some polenta left over – use for another meal. Sprinkle with the combined Pecorino Romano and fontina, spoon over the remaining bechamel, and the remaining tomatoes. Bake for 50 minutes, or until bubbling. Serve in deep, heated plates.

Serves 6-8

Polenta with sausage, ham and pancetta
Polenta invernale

What more could you want on a blustery winter night? Fabulous, quick and easy! Serve with a big, green salad.

10 ounces homemade sausage (see page 240), crumbled, or 2 Italian pork sausages, skin removed, crumbled
4 ounces ham, chopped
2 ounces pancetta, chopped
2 teaspoons chopped rosemary leaves
2 large cloves garlic, finely chopped
1 quantity soft polenta, (see page 86) or 1-minute polenta, freshly made
parmesan cheese, to serve

Preheat the oven to 425°F. Combine the sausage, ham, pancetta, rosemary and garlic in a bowl and mix well.

Pour the polenta into an oiled baking dish or individual dishes and sprinkle with the sausage mixture, pressing it in lightly. Bake 15 minutes, or until the meat mixture is browned and bubbly. Serve hot, in deep heated plates, with parmesan separately.

Serves 4

Farro and vegetable soup with pancetta
Minestra di farro

It's hardly an exaggeration to say the ancient Romans kept whole armies in tip-top shape on farro (similar to spelt), an ancient grain, used in breads, porridge and soups. The grain lost popularity after the introduction of wheat, but recently enthusiasm has been rekindled. These days, farro is primarily grown in Tuscany and Abruzzo.

Farro is available in healthfood stores and organic stores. If difficult to find, substitute with spelt, wheat berries or pearl barley.

1 heaped tablespoon rosemary leaves
2 ounces pancetta, coarsely chopped
2 large cloves garlic, peeled and coarsely chopped
3 tablespoons extra virgin olive oil
10 ounces homemade sausage, crumbled (see page 240), or 2 Italian-type coarse pork sausages, skin
  removed and crumbled
1 onion, chopped
1 large carrot, chopped
1 stalk celery, chopped
14-ounce can cherry tomatoes, with their juice, or roma tomatoes, chopped, with their juice
1 cup red wine
1¼ cup farro (soaked overnight)
grated Pecorino Romano cheese, to serve
crusty bread, to serve

Combine the rosemary, pancetta and garlic in a processor and whiz until you have a paste. Transfer to a small bowl and set aside.

Combine the oil, crumbled sausage, onion, carrot and celery in a large pot and cook over moderate heat until the meat is no longer raw. Stir in the tomatoes, wine and 9 cups of water and bring to a simmer.

Stir in the farro and return to a simmer. Cook gently until the farro is tender, about 40 minutes. Add the reserved rosemary, pancetta and garlic paste, stirring until the paste has dissolved in the soup. Check seasoning and serve in deep, heated plates with Pecorino Romano and bread.

Serves 6

Barley soup with butternut squash and curly endive
Minestra di orzo con zucca

Bring on the cooler weather! This robust soup from the Umbrian countryside is a joy to make and it freezes beautifully – why not make a big batch for future instant wellbeing. Barley works well here, but so will farro or spelt if available.

3 tablespoons extra virgin olive oil
2 large cloves garlic, chopped
1 large onion, chopped
1 large sprig of sage
1 cup pearl barley
1 medium butternut squash, peeled, seeded and cut into ½-¾-inch cubes
10 cups chicken, veal or vegetable stock, or broth (see page 223)
4 cups curly endive or chicory, cut into ½-inch strips

Combine the oil and garlic in a large pot over moderate heat and cook until the garlic is fragrant, about 3 minutes, stirring frequently. Add the onion and sage and sauté until the onion is soft and light golden, about 8 minutes. Stir in the barley and sauté 1 minute in the mixture. Add the butternut squash and sauté 10 minutes.

Stir in the stock and bring to a boil. Season with salt and pepper and simmer very gently, uncovered, until the barley and butternut squash are cooked, about 50 minutes. Remove the sage. Stir in the endive and simmer another 5 minutes or until the endive is tender. Check seasoning and ladle into heated bowls.

Serves 6

Beans & Legumes

Cranberry bean, speck and sauerkraut soup
La jota

La jota *has its origins in Trieste, the small province on the border of the former Yugoslavia, of which it was once a part for a short period. The cooking here is reminiscent of Austria and Hungary, but in essence it's very much Italian. Robust, with beans, speck and sauerkraut, this delicious soup is surprisingly delicate in taste, with the sauerkraut flavor mellowed by gentle cooking.*

During the First World War the Italian troups stationed around Trieste were kept in fighting fit condition on this soup, ready for battle! I love to serve La jota *in colder months, but it freezes well and occasionally I defrost a container on a chilly spring night when a little comfort seems in order.*

1½ tablespoons extra virgin olive oil
5 ounces smoked speck, tough rind removed, meat cut into small cubes
1 small red onion, chopped
2 cloves garlic, finely chopped
3 tablespoons chopped flat-leaf parsley
1 bay leaf
1 sprig fresh sage
1 cup dried cranberry beans, soaked overnight (see page 108)
6 cups water
½ pound sauerkraut, briefly rinsed in a colander
2 medium waxy potatoes, such as red potatoes, peeled and cut into ½-inch cubes

Combine the oil, speck and onion in a large pot and cook over moderately low heat until until the fat runs, the speck browns and the onion is soft, about 10 minutes, stirring frequently. Stir in the garlic, parsley, bay leaf and sage and continue stirring 1 minute more.

Add the beans, water and salt. Cover the pot and bring the water to a simmer over low heat. Simmer 40 minutes, or until the beans are tender. Remove the bay leaf and discard.

Stir in the sauerkraut and potatoes and continue simmering until the potatoes are tender and the soup has thickened slightly, about 20-30 minutes. Check seasoning and serve immediately in deep, heated bowls.

Serves 4

Chickpea and pasta soup
Pasta e ceci

Pasta e ceci *is a Roman institution, no doubt about it. In days past, you would expect it on the menu in authentic Roman establishments on Tuesday, just as* bollito *(boiled beef) would be served on Monday, potato gnocchi on Thursday, pasta with broccoli or salt cod on Friday, tripe on Saturday and suckling lamb* (abbacchio) *on Sunday. Wednesday was the day anything was allowed.*

1½ cups chickpeas, soaked overnight (see page 108)
1 large waxy potato, such as red potato, unpeeled
1 bay leaf
3 tablespoons extra virgin olive oil
1 onion, chopped
two 14-ounce cans Italian cherry tomatoes, or canned diced roma tomatoes
pinch chili flakes
1 pound long pasta, such as linguine, broken into short pieces (to fit a spoon)

Prosciutto and herb battuto
1 ounce slice of fatty prosciutto
6 large basil leaves
¼ cup flat-leaf parsley leaves
2 cloves garlic, peeled

Drain the soaked chickpeas and combine in a pan with the whole potato, a pinch of salt and bay leaf. Add enough water to come up 2-inch above the peas. Cover the pan and bring very slowly to a simmer. Reduce the heat and simmer gently until the potato is tender, about 40 minutes. Remove the potatoes from the pan, peel and puree it. Stir back into the pan.

Meanwhile, combine the oil and onion in a frying pan and cook over moderate heat until soft, about 5 minutes. Drain the tomatoes. Add the juice to the pot with the chickpeas and add the tomatoes to the frying pan. Stir in the chili flakes and season with salt. Cook over moderate heat, stirring frequently, about 10 minutes. Stir this mixture into the cooked chickpeas and simmer 10 minutes.

Cook the pasta in a large pot of boiling, salted water for 5 minutes. Drain, reserving a small measuring cup of the cooking water. Add the pasta to the chickpeas and simmer another 6-10 minutes, or until the pasta is al dente. Stir frequently, so the pasta doesn't stick to the bottom.

Combine all ingredients for the prosciutto and herb battuto on a board or in a small processor and chop finely. Stir into the soup and check seasoning. If the soup is too thick, add enough of the pasta cooking liquid to moisten. Serve in deep, heated plates.

Serves 6

Lentil and rice soup
Minestra di riso e lenticchie

The best lentils in Italy are grown in Castelluccio in Umbria. These are as good as the French lentils from Puy, and certainly no less expensive. The cuisine of Umbria is basically mountain food – capable of filling people up with healthy, sustaining dishes – its use of herbs and spices in complete harmony, without jarring flavors.

In this fabulous soup much of the flavor comes from pancetta, which may be replaced with prosciutto. If feeding vegetarians, the meat may be left out altogether. It will taste different but will still be delicious.

You can make this soup ahead of time, but don't add the rice until just before serving, or the rice will absorb all the liquid, and you'll end up with an unappetizing, grey-looking, mushy mess.

1¼ cup green or brown lentils
10 cups water
1 bay leaf (optional)
1½ tablespoons extra virgin olive oil
4 large cloves garlic, finely chopped
¼ pound pancetta, chopped
1½ tablespoons chopped sage leaves
14-ounce can Italian diced tomatoes, with juice
½ cup arborio rice
2 teaspoons salt
½ cup chopped flat-leaf parsley

Rinse the lentils and place them in a large saucepan. Add the water and bay leaf, bring to a boil, then reduce the heat and simmer, uncovered, for 12 minutes.

Meanwhile, combine the oil and garlic in a deep sauté pan and cook over moderately low heat until the garlic softens, about 3-4 minutes. Add the pancetta and sauté a few minutes, or until the fat runs and the garlic is very soft. Add the sage and tomatoes and their liquid, and simmer 5 minutes to amalgamate flavors.

Pour the tomato mixture into the lentil pan, bring to a boil, then stir in rice and salt. Cook over moderate heat, uncovered, until the lentils and rice are tender, about another 15 minutes. Season with pepper and stir in the parsley. Serve in heated bowls.

Serves 6

Tuscan minestrone
La ribollita

Ribollita (lit. boiled again) is possibly the ultimate in bean soups or minestrone. In Tuscany, black kale (cavolo nero) is a given in ribollita. If not available, use another cabbage, such as savoy, or green leaves such as Swiss chard or chicory.

For the beans
1¼ cups dried cannellini or
  great northern beans, soaked
  overnight (see page 108)
small bunch fresh sage
2 large cloves garlic, bruised with
  the flat side of a chef's knife
1½ tablespoons extra virgin olive oil

For the soup
2 ounces fatty pancetta, finely chopped
1 hot dried chili, chopped, seeds
  removed, if you like
3 tablespoons extra virgin olive oil
1 large red onion, sliced
2 ripe tomatoes, peeled, seeded and
  coarsely chopped

2 large potatoes, such as red potatoes,
  cut into small cubes
2 medium carrots, cut into small cubes
4 celery stalks, cut into small cubes
1 cup stringless green beans, cut
  into ¾-inch pieces
¾ pound black kale, cut into ½-inch strips
1 piece parmesan cheese rind, about 2 ounces
2 large cloves garlic, coarsely chopped
small handful thyme sprigs, coarsely
  chopped

To finish the soup
1 red onion, thinly sliced
thick slices Italian-type bread, such
  as *pane di casa*
2 large cloves garlic, halved

Cook the beans (see page 108) with the addition of sage, garlic, salt and oil. Remove the beans from the liquid and whiz half of the beans in a processor until you have a coarse puree. Reserve the remaining beans in the fridge overnight. Pour the bean cooking liquid into a large measuring jug, and use additional water to make 6 cups.

To make the soup, combine the pancetta, chili and oil in a large pot and cook over low heat until fragrant, about 3 minutes. Add the onion, season with a little salt, and sauté 10 minutes, or until golden. Add the tomatoes and cook a few minutes, then stir in the bean puree. Stir a few minutes, then add the potatoes, carrots, celery, beans, black kale, parmesan rind, garlic and thyme. Add the reserved bean liquid to the pot and bring to a boil. Reduce the heat to low, cover with a lid, and cook 2 hours. Check seasoning and set aside overnight in a cool place.

To finish the soup, preheat the oven to 350°F. Stir the reserved beans into the soup, then spread a layer of thinly sliced onion over the top, transfer the pot to the oven and bake, uncovered, until the onion on top is tender, about 1 hour.

Grill the bread on both sides on a stove-top chargriller and rub with the cut sides of the garlic. Place the bread in heated soup bowls and ladle the hot soup over. Serve with best quality olive oil at the table – traditionally to "baptise the ribollita" with the letter C (said to be for Cristo) .

Serves 6

Classic bean soup
Zuppa di fagioli

Never has there been a soup simpler to make, nor more delicious or comforting. Make up big batches and freeze for instant warmth and sustenance. When I made this for photography not long ago, the whole pan disappeared before my eyes. The fact that it was a sweltering day in the middle of summer seemed to make no difference, although I have to admit that by the time we were eating, the soup wasn't hot any more, just tepid. In Italy, soups such as these are often enjoyed at room temperature in summer.

1 large onion, chopped
2 large carrots, scraped and chopped
3 tablespoons extra virgin olive oil, plus extra for the table
2 large cloves garlic, chopped
2 cups dried cannellini or great northern beans, soaked overnight (see page 108)
10 cups water
handful thyme sprigs
handful flat-leaf parsley, chopped
crusty bread, to serve

Combine the onion, carrots and oil in a large pan and cook over moderate heat until the vegetables are soft, about 10 minutes, stirring frequently. Add the garlic and stir 1 minute more.

Drain the beans, add to the pan, and add water, a good pinch of salt, thyme and parsley. Cover with a lid and bring to a simmer over very low heat. Set the lid at an angle and cook 40-60 minutes or until the beans are very soft. If you like a thicker soup, crush a few tablespoons of the beans against the side of the pan with a wooden spoon. Alternatively, if the soup is too thick, add some hot water. Season with salt and pepper. Serve in deep, heated bowls, with crusty bread and a bottle of good oil on the table.

Serves 6

Dried beans, chickpeas and lentils

SOAKING DRIED BEANS

Dried beans and chickpeas benefit from overnight (or 6-8 hours) soaking in water to cut down on cooking time. Lentils may be cooked without soaking. The volume of beans and chickpeas will increase 2½-3 times, so make sure you cover them with plenty of water to allow for expansion, at least 3 cups of water for every cup of beans.

If you don't have enough time, you can use the "quick-soak" method: cover the beans in a pot with 3 times their volume of water and bring to a boil over high heat. Boil 1-2 minutes, remove from the heat and cover with a lid. Let stand 1 hour, then drain and use as required. This method is effective, but not as gentle as overnight soaking, and the beans' skins may burst.

SALT

My greatest culinary discovery of recent years concerns the "beans and salt" issue. I firmly believed that salt in cooking dried beans was a total no-no: pundits insist that it will make the skins tough and the beans will take much longer to cook.

I set up a side-by-side experiment, salting one batch of cannellini beans, even during soaking, and one lot of identical beans without salt. I drained and rinsed both after soaking, then cooked them, adding salt to the ones that had been soaked with salt, cooking the others without salt.

Lo and behold, both beans cooked in exactly the same time, and furthermore, the beans which had been cooked without salt needed a lot of salt added after cooking, whereas the beans which had been cooked with a modicum of salt to begin with were flavorsome throughout and needed no extra. And the incomparable Marcella Hazan ... in her book *Marcella says* ... agrees!

So much for the myth. I've since cooked all dried beans in this way.

COOKING DRIED BEANS

To cook the soaked beans, drain them from their soaking water and rinse them under cold running water. Put them in a pot with fresh water to cover generously (the beans have probably swollen to their full extent). Add salt sparingly, and any other flavorings, such as a splash of extra virgin olive oil, a sprig of sage and a few peeled garlic cloves, bruised with the flat side of a cook's knife. Cover with a lid and set over the lowest possible heat. When the water starts to simmer, set the lid at an angle and cook over very low heat until the beans are tender. Start checking after 20-30 minutes – they're done if you can squash them flat between your fingers.

Bringing beans to a simmer ever so slowly, and cooking them gently, ensures unbroken skins (even for delicate, thin-skinned lima beans) and tender, but never mushy beans. If not using the beans immediately, reserve them in their cooking liquid.

CANNED BEANS

I don't use canned beans, but if you must, make sure to rinse them several times to avoid the unpleasant metallic "canned" flavor.

Fava beans with smoked pork
Favata

Imagine a winter evening, an open fire, a cushiony couch to curl up on. Serve this robust bean dish to good friends, with a bottle of full-bodied red wine and chunks of crusty bread.

1 smoked ham hock
3 tablespoons extra virgin olive oil
1 small onion, chopped
1¼ pounds pork spareribs, skin removed, cut into ¾-inch pieces
1½ cups dried fava beans, soaked overnight (see page 108)
1 large clove garlic, chopped
2 pounds savoy cabbage, core removed, cut into 4 wedges, each wedge broken in half
4 cups water

Place the ham hock in a pot, large enough to contain all the ingredients later. Cover with water and bring to a boil. Boil over moderately high heat for 15 minutes. Drain and set aside.

Heat the oil in the pot over moderately high heat, add the onion and cook 3 minutes, or until golden brown. Remove from the pot with a slotted spoon and set aside. Add the pork rib pieces to the pan and brown on all sides, about 8 minutes. Reduce the heat to moderately low, return the onion and ham hock, cover the pot and cook another 10 minutes.

Drain the fava beans and add to the pot, together with the garlic, cabbage and the water. Bring to a boil over moderately high heat, then reduce the heat to moderately low and set the lid on an angle. Simmer until the meat is very tender and the fava beans are soft, about 2 hours.

Remove the ham hock from the pot and set aside until cool enough to handle. Pull off the skin, then remove the meat from the bones. Tear meat into bite-sized pieces and stir into the pot. Season with salt and pepper and serve in deep, heated plates.

Serves 4-6

Lima beans with fennel and salami
Fagioli con finocchio e salame

Simple, but big on flavor. The quick-soak method (see page 108) works with most dried beans and legumes, but I don't recommend it for lima beans. These large beans have a very fragile skin and the quick-soak tends to tear it to pieces. Soak the beans overnight and then cook them as slowly as possible, so that they swell gently and stay safely contained within their silky overcoats. They are great served warm with meat, such as roast pork fillets or lamb cutlets, or cold as a salad.

2½ cups dried lima beans or any other dried white beans, soaked overnight (see page 108)
2 large cloves garlic, bruised with the side of a cook's knife, plus 1 large clove, finely chopped
few sprigs sage
extra virgin olive oil
1½ tablespoons red wine vinegar, plus 6 tablespoons extra
¼ large fennel bulb, thinly sliced
½ medium red onion, thinly sliced into half-moons
¼ pound sopressa salami, thickly sliced and chopped

Cook the beans by the slowest possible method (see above) with 2 cloves garlic, sage and a splash of olive oil and a pinch of salt.

Meanwhile, combine 1½ tablespoons red wine vinegar with a good pinch of salt in a bowl and whisk until the salt has dissolved. Add the fennel and onion and toss well. Set aside.

When the beans are tender, drain them and toss with 6 tablespoons red wine vinegar, 1 finely chopped clove garlic, and season with salt and pepper. To serve warm, gently stir in the fennel and onion, and the salami. Serve with a bottle of the finest extra virgin olive oil at the table.

If you like to serve this as a salad, leave the beans to cool after adding the vinegar, garlic and seasoning, and then adding the fennel, onion and salami when cool.

Serves 6

Salads & Vegetables

Winter salad with walnuts
Insalata invernale

This is one of the recipes nearly everyone in my classes has made at home time after time. A mandoline – a gadget with a dangerously sharp blade – makes slicing the fennel, cabbage and radicchio a breeze. Walnut oil in the dressing underlines the walnut flavor, but if you don't have it in your pantry, use the same quantity of extra virgin olive oil. Always a winner, serve as a starter to a rich winter meal.

1 large fennel bulb, cut into quarters and thinly sliced
¼ savoy cabbage, thinly sliced
1 large radicchio, cut into quarters and thinly sliced, including the core
2 heads Belgian endive, thinly sliced (optional)
¼ pound walnuts, lightly toasted and coarsely chopped
¼ pound prosciutto, grilled until slightly crisp
½ cup parmesan cheese shavings

Dressing
3 tablespoons red wine vinegar
good pinch of salt
¼ cup extra virgin olive oil
¼ cup walnut oil

Make the dressing first: combine the vinegar and salt in a large bowl and whisk until the salt has been dissolved. Drizzle in the oils, whisking constantly, until the mixture thickens. Check seasoning.

Add the fennel, cabbage, radicchio and Belgian endive to the dressing and toss well. Spread on a large platter and scatter with the walnuts, prosciutto and parmesan. Serve immediately.

Serves 6

Bell pepper salad with capers
Peperoni arrostiti con capperi

Versatile bell peppers are widely used all over Italy, from the north to the south, and they can be served hot or cold, on their own or to accompany meats or fish. Red and yellow varieties have the best flavor – better than green, which is more acidic. Serve this salad as a starter, with plenty of crusty bread.

4 large bell peppers, choose any one color, or a mixture
1 large tomato, finely chopped
1 clove garlic, finely chopped
handful basil leaves, torn
handful mint leaves, torn
¼ cup extra virgin olive oil
1½ tablespoons capers, rinsed

Preheat broiler.

Quarter the bell peppers lengthwise, remove membranes and seeds and place on a broiler rack, skin side up. Broil until skins have blackened all over. Remove from rack and place in a bowl. Cover with plastic wrap and let stand 20 minutes to "sweat."

Meanwhile, combine tomato, garlic, basil, mint and oil in a bowl, mix well and season with salt and pepper.

Rub skin off the bell peppers, cut flesh into strips and place in a bowl. Mix with the tomato dressing, cover and refrigerate 1 hour. Serve immediately, scattered with capers.

Serves 6

Arugula and radicchio salad
Insalata di rucola e radicchio

Pretty as a picture, this salad comes up trumps in big flavors and texture. Serve as a starter before a winter meal.

6 cups baby arugula, rinsed and spun-dry
1 large radicchio, leaves rinsed and spun-dry, thinly shredded
½ cup drained sun-dried tomatoes in oil, thinly sliced
2 tablespoons freshly squeezed lemon juice
¼ cup extra virgin olive oil
½ cup slivered almonds, lightly toasted
1½ cups smoked mozzarella cheese, cut into bite-sized pieces

Combine the arugula, radicchio and tomatoes in a large bowl. In a small bowl, combine the lemon juice with a good pinch of salt and whisk until salt has dissolved. Gradually add the oil, whisking constantly, until the mixture emulsifies. Check seasoning. Add the almonds and smoked mozzarella and toss well before serving.

Serves 6

Tuscan splendor
and a mouthful of sand

We left Rome for Tuscany, hiring a car with our friends and my sister. The autostrada *passes through Umbria and takes in spectacular views of fortified hilltop villages. We'd rented our holiday villa in advance but we didn't know how great it would be.*

We arrived in hot sunshine and were welcomed in a shady courtyard with a tray of chilled wine and olives. The old monastery of San Niccolo d'Olmeto is 1,000 years old, with a chapel and a signal tower that was a link in the medieval communications between Florence and Rome. "La Signora" and her son, Giovanni, who now own the place, have created a grand home and attractive accommodation for guests.

Our apartment was on two levels, with three-feet-thick walls, terra cotta floors and a generous balcony. It was perfect. But the rudimentary kitchen left something to be desired, and the same went for our friends' kitchen. Their oven didn't work but their stove top did; our stove top didn't but the oven did; they had one frying pan; we had a saucepan. Between us we managed just fine.

We did buy a knife from a local store, and in fact we ate brilliantly.

One night, La Signora invited us to have dinner with her and Giovanni and their friends. They set up a barbecue grill in a mini amphitheatre in the olive grove, and we ate fabulous porridgy *panzanella* (see page 266), arugula salad from the garden, and two-fingers thick T-bone steaks of the famous Val di Chiana beef, sliced into hearty strips and served with lemon wedges. The meal – like the Signora – was essentially Tuscan, elegant in its austerity.

But there was nothing austere about the hospitality. After the meal, Giovanni invited us in for drinks and introduced us to his private collection of grappa. All over Italy, as soon as a guest comes into your home, the grappa bottle is out on the table. The custom was well honored that night.

We came across more grappa in the pretty market town of Greve in Chianti. The *enoteca* (wine merchant) has a sizeable room that's a shrine for grappa, all in different bottles, each more fanciful than the last. Grappa can be expensive these days but, in fact, it's typical of *cucina povera* – a drink distilled in northern vineyards from what's left after the grapes are pressed for wine. For centuries it has warmed the chill winters.

There are outstanding shops in the town square in Greve, including a butcher, a baker and a deli, where we found the Umbrian lentils of Castellucio and a beautiful fresh (*dolce*) Pecorino cheese. The *norcineria* had a lovely smoky smell, and was stacked from floor to ceiling with pork specialities of the region: sausages, hams, coppa, and other cured meats. We bought corn-yellow chicken wrapped in pancetta there for dinner (see page 206), and at the bakery the distinctive saltless bread of Tuscany.

On days when we wanted to relax, we would make a simple pasta lunch at San Niccolo and set a table under the fruit trees. Tuscany was perfection, but it's sometimes forgotten that this region, like most of Italy, was not always a land of plenty. *Mangiafagioli*, or "bean-eaters" as Tuscans are nicknamed, have had it rough over the years. The cycle of the seasons makes every crop special, and many have their own *sagra* (festival) to celebrate. We were there at the time of the porcini *sagra* and for breakfast on our last morning we pan-fried some with garlic and parsley. Unfortunately, the "cook" forgot how gritty these mushrooms can be. We ended up with delicious flavor and mouthfuls of sand.

Potato, beet and cannellini bean salad
Insalata di patate e barbietiole

The beets color this whole salad a delightful pink, but if you like to keep colors separate, add the beets last and place them strategically by hand. This salad is good on its own as a side dish, or as a base for pan-fried fish or chicken breast.

2 cups dried cannellini or great northern beans, soaked overnight or
 quick-soaked (see page 108)
1 large red onion, finely chopped
½ cup extra virgin olive oil
⅓ cup red wine vinegar
4 large red beets, boiled or roasted, peeled and cubed
16 fingerling or pink fir apple potatoes, or 4 large red potatoes, boiled in their skin and
 cut into bite-sized pieces

Drain the soaked beans and place in a clean pot with fresh water to cover. Bring slowly to a simmer and cook until the beans are tender, about 30-60 minutes, depending on age of beans.

Drain and while still warm, combine in a large bowl with the onion, oil, vinegar, beets and potatoes. Season with salt and pepper and serve immediately or at room temperature.

Serves 6

Arugula salad with pear and Pecorino
Insalata di rucola

Start an autumn dinner with this light but flavorful salad. Make sure the pear is not over-ripe and still has a good crunchy texture.

1½ tablespoons sherry vinegar or red wine vinegar
¼ cup extra virgin olive oil
1 small french shallot, finely chopped
4 cups arugula leaves
1 small fennel bulb, thinly sliced (optional)
1 ripe, but firm pear, cored and thinly sliced
¼ cup coarsely chopped flat-leaf parsley leaves
1 cup shaved Pecorino Romano or parmesan cheese

Combine the vinegar and a good pinch of salt in a bowl and whisk until the salt has dissolved. Add the oil slowly, whisking constantly, until the dressing thickens. Stir in the shallot.

Combine arugula, fennel, pear and parsley in a salad bowl and toss. Add dressing and toss again. Top with the shaved cheese and serve immediately.

Serves 4-6

Warm potato salad with celery
Insalata di patate calde

A very popular vegetable dish in Rome's trattorias, but no less so in Tuscany and Umbria, where celery is highly regarded.

2 pounds floury (Yukon gold or russet) potatoes, scrubbed and halved or quartered
¼ cup extra virgin olive oil
¼ cup chopped flat-leaf parsley
tender and pale inner stalks of 1 head celery, with leaves, chopped

Cover the potatoes in a pan with water. Bring to a boil, add salt, then cook over moderate heat until potatoes are just tender, 20-30 minutes, depending on size. Drain and cool a few minutes. Peel and cut into bite-sized pieces.

While potatoes are still warm, toss them in a bowl with oil, parsley and celery. Season with salt and plenty of pepper. Serve immediately.

Serves 4

Asparagus and provolone gratin
Asparagi gratinati

Don't cook the asparagus any longer than necessary, just until they're bright green and crisp-tender. Serve as a starter or for lunch with a salad.

2 bunches asparagus, woody bottom ends snapped off
¼ pound provolone cheese, thinly sliced
3 tablespoons freshly grated parmesan cheese
extra virgin olive oil

Preheat a broiler.

Plunge the asparagus into a pot of salted, boiling water. Cook 3-6 minutes, depending on their thickness. Drain and place in a baking dish. Arrange the provolone over the stalks, avoiding the heads. Scatter with parmesan and drizzle liberally with oil. Season with freshly ground black pepper.

Broil the asparagus until the cheese starts to melt. Serve on heated plates.

Serves 4

Chicory with garlic and chili
Cicoria strascinati

Any greens, but especially bitter greens, can be used for this method of cooking, which is virtually mandatory in trattorias. Try it with broccoli raab, curly endive, Swiss chard or spinach. The tender leaves of spinach don't need parboiling before being added to the garlic, oil and chili.

I large bunch chicory (1¾ pounds) tough stems removed
3 tablespoons extra virgin olive oil
2 large cloves garlic, finely chopped
¼ teaspoon chili flakes

Bring 12-16 cups of water to a boil in a large pot. Add chicory with a good pinch of salt and boil 4 minutes. Drain in a colander and squeeze to remove excess liquid. Chop coarsely. You should have about 4 cups.

Heat the oil in a large frying pan over moderate heat. Add garlic and chili, and sauté 1-2 minutes, until garlic is fragrant. Add chicory and sauté 3-4 minutes. Serve immediately.

Serves 4

Cavolo nero

Chicory

Broccoli raab

Curly endive

Greens

Radicchio

Swiss chard

Arugula

Belgian endive

These are some of my favorite vegetables. All true bitter greens belong to the chicory family. Among bitter greens you can also count arugula, although it's really more peppery than bitter, and radicchio, which is not green but red. Chicory, curly endive, broccoli raab and Belgian endive (white leaf, which also has a red variety) all give great umph and added interest to a dish, be it pasta, risotto, soups or stews. Watercress, with its peppery flavor, is often used in much the same ways in Italian recipes. All bitter greens can be eaten raw or cooked.

Savoy cabbage soup with cannellini beans
Minestra di cavoli con fagioli

Despite hearty and wintry flavors, this soup is surprisingly delicate. If you have meat essence, it enriches the texture and flavor incredibly well – if not, it's still well and truly a cut above the average.

1 medium savoy cabbage
¼ cup extra virgin olive oil
2 large cloves garlic, finely chopped
2 teaspoons rosemary leaves
2 ounces pancetta, chopped
3 cups cooked cannellini or great northern beans (see page 108)
4 tablespoons meat essence (see page 220, optional)
thick slices of Italian-style bread, such as *pane di casa* or ciabatta, toasted
grated parmesan cheese, to serve (optional)

Shred the cabbage finely. A mandoline will make this very quick and easy, or you can slice it with a sharp knife on a board .

Combine the oil, garlic, rosemary and pancetta in a large soup pot and cook over moderate heat until the pancetta fat runs and the garlic is fragrant, about 4 minutes. Add the cabbage, season with salt, and stir until coated, about 5 minutes. Add 16 cups water, set a lid securely on top, and set over low heat. Leave to cook undisturbed for 3 hours.

Stir in the cannellini beans and meat essence, if using, and cook, uncovered another 30 minutes.

To serve, place a slice of toast in deep, heated bowls, spoon the soup over the toast and serve immediately, with parmesan, if you like.

Serves 8-12

Baked sweet potatoes with taleggio
Patate dolci al forno

Centuries before the common potato, as we know it, found acceptance in Italy, sweet potatoes were very popular all over Europe, and were, indeed, the only potato. Not until the late 18th century was there any mention of "sweet potato" in an English dictionary, thus distinguishing it from the potato we now recognize as a household staple. In those early days, the flavor of the sweet potato would be further enhanced with extra sugar, spices and dried fruit, but in Italy in the Veneto region they got the right idea and added fabulous taleggio cheese, making this recipe one you'll treasure forever.

2 sweet potatoes, scrubbed
1½ tablespoons unsalted butter, plus 3 tablespoons extra, at room temperature
½ small onion, finely chopped
1 teaspoon chopped thyme leaves, plus extra sprigs
1 large egg
¼ cup taleggio or fontina cheese, chopped

Preheat the oven to 400°F. Bake the sweet potatoes on a baking paper-lined baking sheet until tender, about 45-60 minutes. Remove from the oven and allow to cool slightly.

Melt 1½ tablespoons butter in a small frying pan over moderate heat. Add onion and sauté until soft, about 2 minutes. Add chopped thyme and cook 1 minute more. Remove from the heat and set aside.

Cut the potatoes in half lengthwise. Spoon out the flesh, leaving a ¾-inch shell of flesh and skin. Place the halves on a baking sheet. Combine the scooped out potato flesh with the remaining 3 tablespoons butter, the onion, egg and taleggio in a bowl and mash until smooth. Season with salt. Pile mixture back into the sweet potato shells, scatter with thyme sprigs, and bake 20-30 minutes, or until golden.

Serves 4

Roman springtime stew
La vignarola

The artichoke is revered in Italy's capital, and used in stews, pastas, risottos, or deep-fried in batter. When it's in the markets, you know spring has arrived.

⅓ cup extra virgin olive oil, plus extra for drizzling
1 large red onion, cut into thick slices
2 large cloves garlic, finely chopped
4 artichokes, prepared and cut into ½-inch vertical slices (see below)
1 large fennel bulb, halved, thickly sliced horizontally
1 pound waxy potatoes, peeled and cut into ¾-inch pieces
1 pound fresh fava beans, shelled
½ pound fresh peas in the pod, shelled
1 bunch chicory, tough stems removed, cut into strips
freshly grated Pecorino cheese, to serve
toasted bread or crusty fresh bread, to serve

Combine the oil and onion in a large sauté pan or sauce pot and cook over moderate heat until soft, about 8 minutes. Add the garlic and cook 1 minute more. Stir in the artichokes and cook a few minutes, and repeat with the fennel and potatoes. Stir in the fava beans and peas, then chicory, and stir until it wilts a little.

Add enough water to just cover the vegetables and season with salt and pepper. Bring to a boil, then reduce heat and simmer over very low heat, half-covered with the lid, until all the vegetables are tender, about 30 minutes, giving the pot an occasional stir. Check the seasoning and serve in heated bowls, with the cheese, extra virgin olive oil separately for drizzling, and plenty of bread to mop up juices.

Serves 4

TO PREPARE ARTICHOKES
To prepare artichokes, have a bowl with acidulated (with lemon juice) water handy. Start pulling away the leaves, starting at the bottom and turning the artichoke around as you go. Keep pulling off the leaves while turning the artichoke in your hand, until you get to the palest green leaves.

Now cut off the stalk level with the choke (or leaving a 2-inch stalk, if you prefer) and the top third of the artichoke (depending on size, about 1½-inch). Rub all the cut and exposed surfaces with a halved lemon.

Hold artichoke in your hand as if you were peeling a potato, and carefully pare away any dark green bits around the bottom, leaving nothing but white, and rubbing with lemon. Cut artichoke in half lengthwise, rub exposed areas with lemon, and with a teaspoon scoop out the hairy choke. Place halved artichoke with the flat, cut side on a chopping board and cut lengthwise into ½-inch slices. Reserve in acidulated water.

Potato pie with smoked mozzarella and salami
Torta di patate

A potato dish with so many different flavors, it's a satisfying meal in itself.
Serve with a tossed green salad for a lunch or light dinner, or take on your next
picnic. You can choose to make it in a springfrom cake tin and unmold it,
this makes it more like a cake. Either way, it is utterly delicious and cheesy!
Smoked mozzarella cheese is available in Italian delis in the chilled compartment,
usually stored next to plain mozzarella.

2½ pounds starchy potatoes, such as Yukon gold
4 tablespoons unsalted butter, plus 1½ tablespoons for the dish, plus another
　1½ tablespoons for the top, melted
⅔ cup freshly grated parmesan cheese
1 cup milk
2 large eggs, lightly beaten
½ pound smoked mozzarella cheese, cut into pea-sized cubes
¼ pound salami, preferably sopresso, chopped
3 tablespoons chopped flat-leaf parsley
¼ pound fresh mozzarella cheese, such as bocconcini, thinly sliced
1 cup fluffy breadcrumbs (see page 273)

Cook the potatoes in salted water until tender. Drain and when cool enough to handle, peel
them and mash in a large bowl. Stir in 4 tablespoons butter and the parmesan, then add the
milk, eggs, smoked mozzarella, salami and parsley. Stir well and season with salt and pepper.

Preheat the oven to 375°F. Use 1½ tablespoons softened butter to grease a pie or gratin dish,
or a 9-inch springform cake pan. Spoon half the potato mixture into the dish and level the
top. Cover with the fresh mozzarella slices, then top with the remaining potato mixture.
Combine the breadcrumbs in a bowl with the melted butter and mix well with your hands.
Sprinkle over the top.

Bake until the top is golden and crunchy and filling is hot and bubbly, about 40 minutes.
Remove from the oven and let stand 10 minutes before releasing the sides of the cake pan.
Serve on a platter, or straight from the dish if you use a pie dish or a gratin dish.

Serves 6

Potato gratin with tomatoes, olives and capers
Gratin di patate

The complex flavors of this gratin makes it an ideal side dish to a plain roasted fish, such as snapper, or a piece of beef.

4 large, ripe tomatoes, peeled, halved and seeded
2 pounds waxy potatoes, such as nicola or red potatoes, peeled and cut into ½-inch thick slices
1½ tablespoons extra virgin olive oil, plus 1½ tablespoons extra
2 red onions, thinly sliced
1 teaspoon thyme leaves, plus a handful of sprigs, extra
⅓ cup pitted and coarsely chopped black olives, preferably kalamata
3 cloves garlic, thinly sliced
½ small lemon, sliced wafer-thin
1½ tablespoons capers, rinsed

Preheat the oven to 400°F.

Chop one of the tomatoes and slice the rest. Plunge the potatoes into a large pot of boiling, salted water and boil 4 minutes. Drain, rinse briefly under cold water and set aside.

Combine 1⅓ tablespoons of the oil in a frying pan with the onions and thyme and season with pepper. Sauté over moderately high heat until the onions start to color, about 8-10 minutes. Arrange them in a lightly oiled gratin dish and scatter with the chopped tomato, the olives, half of the garlic, half of the thyme sprigs and half of the lemon. Make layers with the potatoes, the sliced tomatoes and the remaining garlic, thyme sprigs and lemon slices and the capers. Season with salt and pepper and drizzle with remaining oil.

Cover with foil and bake 30 minutes. Remove the foil and bake another 20-30 minutes, or until potatoes are very tender. Let stand at room temperature for 5 minutes before serving.

Serves 6

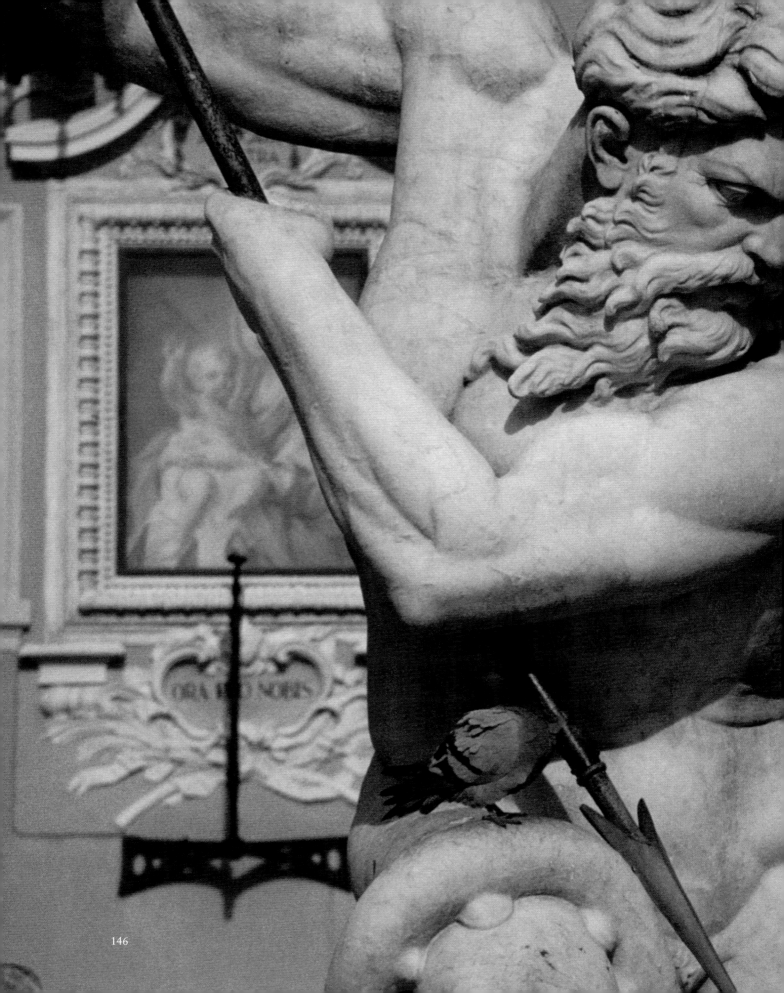

Eggs & Cheese

Egg ramekins
Uova in cocotte

Serve these eggs for breakfast, brunch or a light lunch. Instead of tomato sauce, mushrooms, lightly cooked, or spinach are a fabulous base for the eggs, or a few tablespoons chopped ham may be added to the tomato sauce. A small baby arugula salad is good served on the side.

extra virgin olive oil
½ cup plain breadcrumbs
1¾ cups homemade tomato sauce (see page 26)
6 large, fresh eggs
½ cup grated or finely chopped fontina cheese
toasted slices of ciabatta, to serve

Preheat the oven to 375°F. Brush the inside of 6 ramekins with oil and sprinkle with breadcrumbs.

Set the ramekins on a baking sheet. Spoon the tomato sauce into the ramekins and break
1 egg into each, scatter with the cheese and bake until the cheese is bubbly and the egg whites have just set, about 10 minutes. Serve immediately with toast.

Serves 6

Frittata with scamorza
Frittata al forno

Scamorza, which is available at Italian deli counters, resembles mozzarella in consistency. Often smoked, this cheese is usually formed into a pear-shape, and sometimes animal shapes. If you can't find it, use plain or smoked mozzarella.

3 tablespoons extra virgin olive oil
4 large eggs, lightly beaten
3 tablespoons freshly grated parmesan cheese
1½ tablespoons chopped flat-leaf parsley
small handful basil leaves, coarsely torn
½ pound scamorza cheese or fresh bocconcini, sliced
1 large roma tomato, thinly sliced

Preheat a broiler.

Heat the oil in a 9-inch non-stick frying pan set over moderately low heat. Meanwhile, combine the eggs, parmesan, parsley and basil in a bowl and season with salt and pepper. Pour the mixture into the pan and cook 5 minutes, or until the bottom has set.

Remove the pan from the heat and divide the scamorza over the top. Scatter with the tomato slices and place under the broiler until the cheese is bubbly and starting to melt, about 3-5 minutes. Let stand a few minutes before serving.

Serves 4

Italian cheese – such as parmesan, and the goat's cheese used on the next page – is indispensable in cooking but there are notable table cheeses too. Gorgonzola, a little Lombardy town about half-an-hour from Milan, has produced its creamy, blue-streaked, cow's milk cheese for over 2000 years.

Swiss chard, red onion and caper frittata
Frittata di bietola

*So often the stalks of Swiss chard (*bietola*) are discarded, while only the glossy, crinkly leaves are used. Here, however, I use the stalks as well as the leaves, in keeping with the* cucina povera *principle of using everything on hand. The stalks provide a slight crunch and great flavor. You can increase the number of eggs to 6, but I prefer a slightly thinner frittata.*

5 stems Swiss chard with leaves (about 7 ounces), stems and leaves separated
2 cloves garlic, finely chopped
1 red onion, thinly sliced
3 tablespoons extra virgin olive oil
2 teaspoons capers, drained
4 large eggs
½ cup goat's cheese, crumbled

Thinly slice the Swiss chard stems and shred the leaves. Combine the Swiss chard stems, the garlic, onion and oil in a non-stick, medium-sized frying pan and cook over moderate heat for a few minutes, stirring frequently. Stir in the shredded leaves and cook another 1-2 minutes, or until the leaves are wilting. Stir in the capers, turn up the heat and stir until any remaining moisture has evaporated.

Preheat a broiler.

Beat the eggs in a bowl and season with salt and pepper. Pour over the vegetables, making sure the egg is well distributed. Cook over moderate heat until the bottom is set and golden and the top is no longer liquid, about 5-10 minutes. Scatter with the goat's cheese, pressing it in lightly. Finish the frittata under the preheated broiler, until the top is firm and the cheese starts to brown. Serve warm or at room temperature.

Serves 4

Poached eggs with parmesan
Uova affogate al parmigiano

I love the elegance and simplicity of this recipe, but I have to stress that poaching eggs will only work satisfactorily with very fresh free range eggs.

12 large, fresh eggs
½ cup freshly grated parmesan cheese
grilled toast, to serve

Preheat oven to 400°F and butter a gratin dish in which the cooked eggs will fit in one layer.

Poach the eggs in batches and transfer to the gratin dish. Sprinkle with salt and pepper and scatter with parmesan. Bake 5 minutes, or until the cheese has melted. Serve immediately with toast.

Serves 6

POACHING EGGS
To poach eggs, bring a large, preferably deep pan of water to a boil. Add salt and a good splash of white vinegar.

Crack the eggs individually into cups or small bowls. When the water is boiling, create a whirlpool by stirring with a wooden spoon. Turn down the heat to simmering, slide in the eggs one by one, and cook until the whites have just set, but the yolks are still runny, about 3 minutes. It's best not to poach more than 3-4 eggs at a time.

Remove with a slotted spoon and drain, on the spoon, on paper towels, then slide gently on to a plate.

Baked cheese and prosciutto omelettes
Omelette di formagio al forno

Fabulous to serve when people come over for brunch or a light lunch. Serve with a mixed green salad.

6 large eggs, lightly beaten
4 tablespoons unsalted butter
¼ cup prosciutto, chopped
¼ cup grated fontina or gruyere cheese, plus 1½ tablespoons extra for the top
3 tablespoons grated parmesan cheese, plus 1½ tablespoons extra for the top

Preheat oven to 400°F and butter a gratin dish large enough to hold the omelettes in one layer.

Break the eggs into a bowl and season with salt. Whisk until the yolk and whites are just combined, but don't overbeat. Heat 1½ tablespoons of the butter in a 7-inch non-stick frying pan and add about 2 generous tablespoons of the eggs. Cook over moderate heat until the underside is golden and set, flip over and lightly cook the other side. Set aside on a plate. Repeat with the remaining mixture, making about 12 small omelettes.

Place the omelettes on a flat surface and scatter each with the prosciutto and a little of the combined cheeses. Roll up and place in the buttered gratin dish. Scatter with the remaining cheeses and bake 10 minutes, or until the cheese has melted.

Serves 4-6

Fish & Seafood

Sweet and sour sardines
Sarde in saor

Serve these sardines as part of an antipasto platter or as a simple starter by themselves. Cooking fish first, then marinating in a sweet-sour mixture, is an age-old Venetian tradition. You can do the same with rainbow trout fillets.

2 pounds fresh sardines, scaled and butterflied
flour, for dusting
3 tablespoons extra virgin olive oil
2 large red onions, sliced
⅓ cup sugar
½ cup slivered almonds
½ cup golden raisins
¼ cup white wine vinegar

Season the sardines with salt and pepper, then dust with flour, shaking off any excess. Heat the oil in a large frying pan and fry the sardines until golden on both sides. Drain on paper towels, then arrange in a single layer in a dish.

Add the onions to the frying pan and cook over moderate heat until soft, about 8 minutes. Stir in the sugar, almonds and golden raisins and stir until the sugar has dissolved. Add the vinegar and stir 1 minute more.

Spoon the sweet and sour mixture over the sardines and let cool. Refrigerate for at least 24 hours. Season well with pepper before serving.

Serves 6 as a starter

TO BUTTERFLY SARDINES
With a small sharp knife open up the belly cavity from vent to gills. Cut off the head. Open up the sardine and rinse inside and out under cold water. Dry well on paper towels.

Place sardines flat on a board, skin side up, and massage the backbone through the skin (this will release the bones from the flesh). Pull away the backbone with the bones attached, from head to tail.

Fish and fennel stew with tomatoes and saffron
Zuppa di pesce al forno

A fabulous one-pot meal: all you need is a green salad to serve afterwards. Leftovers freeze very well. There is a certain similarity with the French bouillabaisse – *such as the presence of saffron – but this is much easier to make, with only one type of fish.*

Friselle *are individual, round dried breads with a hole in the middle. For centuries, Neapolitan sailors used to take these to sea to enrich stews such as this one.*

¼ teaspoon saffron threads
2 pounds thick fish fillets, such as snapper, cod or kingfish, cut into 1½-inch pieces
1½ tablespoons extra virgin olive oil, plus 3 tablespoons extra, plus enough oil to drizzle
freshly squeezed juice of ½ lemon
2 medium red onions, sliced
1 large fennel bulb, sliced
3 large cloves garlic, finely chopped
½ cup coarsely chopped flat-leaf parsley
1½ tablespoons chopped fresh oregano
2 large tomatoes, peeled, seeded and coarsely chopped
¼ teaspoon chili flakes (optional)
1 cup dry white wine
4 friselle or thick slices Italian-type bread, such as *pane di casa* or ciabatta, grilled

Place the saffron in a small bowl and pour over 1½ tablespoons hot water. Set aside at least 20 minutes, or until needed.

Place the fish in a dish in one layer. Pour over 1½ tablespoons olive oil, squeeze over the lemon juice and season with salt. Turn fish over to coat on both sides and season the other side with salt. Cover with plastic wrap and refrigerate for 2 hours or until needed.

Preheat the oven to 350°F. Combine 3 tablespoons oil, onions and fennel in a large, heavy-based pan which can accommodate the fish later in one layer. Sauté over moderate heat until vegetables are soft, about 5-8 minutes. Stir in garlic, parsley and oregano and cook another 2 minutes. Stir in tomatoes, chili flakes, if used, wine, reserved saffron and its soaking liquid, and remove the pan from the heat.

Arrange the fish in one layer on top of the other ingredients. Season lightly with salt and pepper. Add enough water to just cover the fish. Drizzle liberally with oil and cover the pot securely. Bake 40 minutes, or until the fish flakes easily when tested with the point of a sharp knife. Check seasoning.

Place friselle in heated, deep plates and ladle the stew over the top. Serve immediately.

Serves 4

Seeing Italy
through a red blur

For me, Italy has almost always meant the happiest of times but there was one spring when I drove the length of the country from Milan to Sicily and saw everything through a red blur: the red of the poppies growing everywhere beside the roads, and the blur of my tears.

The trip was planned as a last-ditch attempt to rescue a failing marriage. We had booked several exciting stops along the way: Fiesole near Florence at the San Michele hotel, which was designed in part by Michelangelo; Siena where by good luck we would be in time to watch the festival of the Palio; Rome at the famous Hassler hotel at the top of the Spanish Steps; Positano on the Bay of Naples across from Capri; and on to the Palace San Domenico hotel at Taormina in Sicily.

But despite the fabulous locations, and great lunches and dinners, nothing could alleviate our unhappiness, and I kept on seeing Italy through the red blur of poppies everywhere.

It happened many years ago but the feelings are as clear to me now as they were then. I remember that the poppies gave me hope for a happier future.

People come home from all over Italy to Siena to celebrate the *Palio* every summer. The 460-year-old horse race is held in the Piazza del Campo, the medieval square, with each of the horsemen representing a "contrada," or neighborhood of the city. I'll never forget the sound of the thundering hooves on the sand-covered piazza. You couldn't help being caught up in the excitement and tension of the race, run at full tilt, with the honor of the contradas at stake. Siena, with its beautiful cathedral, is also home to enduring food traditions. *Panforte* has been made here since the Middle Ages; translated as "strong bread," it is a spicy, flat cake that keeps for a long time. It's a Christmas treat, though it's made in Siena year round, and of course it has traveled all over the world. There's no recipe for it in this book, it's certainly not cucina povera – besides, how could I hope to compete with centuries of Sienese expertise. Look for *panforte* in your local deli.

The first time in my life that I saw fireflies was walking back up the hill to San Michele one sultry July night. Years later, near Greve in Chianti, where we were staying with friends, there they were again.

Having grown up in northern Europe, I thought fireflies were the stuff of fairy tales. Magic.

Taormina, a small town on the east coast of Sicily, holds a touching memory for me. High on the hill, out of the way at the top of a winding road, is a little caffè, Bar San Giorgio. Here, during the invasion of Italy in 1944, the allied leaders, Churchill and Mountbatten among them, used to meet. For me, it was strange to sit and look out to the tranquil Mediterranean and think of the drama that had happened there. As I mention elsewhere, it was in Taormina that I made some new kitchen friends. Sicilian food, I learned, reflects the history of the ancient island, with its unique mix of spices and seafood, and the exotic influence of Saracens and Greeks and North Africans.

I do love poppies and happy times did come again. Many years later, my friend Pat and I left our car by the roadside in a Tuscan lane and gathered armfuls of wild red poppies. Back at our holiday villa we put them in vases. They lasted for a week, still fresh and beautiful on the day we left to drive to Rome.

Trout with lemon and parsley butter sauce
Trota al burro

Things don't get much simpler, but with the freshest trout and good butter, this is sublime! Feel free to use the same method with different whole fish or fillets. Serve with boiled potatoes and a green salad.

6 whole small rainbow trout, about ½ pound each
flour, for dredging
¼ cup extra virgin olive oil
6 tablespoons unsalted butter
¼ cup freshly squeezed lemon juice
½ cup light chicken stock or broth (see page 223)
¼ cup finely chopped flat-leaf parsley

Set the oven to the lowest possible temperature. Rinse the trout inside and out and dry on paper towels. Dust the trout with flour, shaking off any excess.

Heat the oil over moderate heat in one large (or 2 medium) frying pans. Add the trout and cook about 6-7 minutes on the first side, then turn and cook another 5-6 minutes on the second side, or until the fish flakes, and comes away from the bone easily when tested with a sharp knife. Transfer the trout to a platter and keep warm in the oven.

Wipe out the pan(s) and add the butter and lemon juice. Cook over low heat until the butter has melted, stirring constantly, about 1-2 minutes, then stir in the chicken stock. Turn up the heat and cook until reduced by half, then stir in the parsley.

Place the fish on heated plates, pour over a little of the sauce and serve immediately.

Serves 6

Fish fillets with beans and tomatoes
Guazzetto di pesce e fagioli

I just love this – a feast every time. It's got all the right elements: simplicity, lightness and great flavor. Serve with forks as well as spoons to get the very last of the fabulous juices – you won't need knives.

3 tablespoons extra virgin olive oil
2 large cloves garlic, finely chopped
¼ teaspoon chili flakes
1 pound cherry tomatoes, halved
1 cup dry white wine
1 cup dried cannellini or great northern beans, cooked (see page 108)
good handful flat-leaf parsley leaves, coarsely chopped
4 white fish fillets, about 6 ounces each (such as cod or snapper) cut into
  2-inch pieces or left whole
lemon wedges and grilled bread, to serve

Heat the oil in a large sauté pan over moderate heat. Add the garlic, chili flakes, tomatoes and wine and simmer until the tomatoes are soft, about 10 minutes. Drain the beans and add them to the pan, together with the parsley, and cook another 5 minutes. Check seasoning.

Lay the fish on top and season with salt. Cover the pan with a lid and cook over low heat until the fish is just cooked through, about another 10-15 minutes, depending on thickness. Serve in deep, heated plates with lemon wedges and grilled bread.

Serves 4

Whole fish with rosemary
Pesce di Andy

Long before I started working with Andy Harris, I lost my heart to this recipe for cooking whole fish in his fabulous book Modern Greek Food. *When asked if I could use the recipe in this book, he agreed without hesitation – such is the generosity in our food world! The fact that the recipe translates so seamlessly from Greek to Italian is due to Italy's occupation by the Greeks over many centuries.*

Any dense, flavorsome fish works well in this recipe – it's a good chance to try inexpensive varieties that need thorough cooking. Please give it a go.

6 whole fish, about ½ pound each (tilapia, catfish or sea bass)
3 tablespoons unsalted butter
3 tablespoons extra virgin olive oil
good handful rosemary sprigs, coarsely chopped
3 tablespoons red wine vinegar
3 tablespoons water

Choose a large frying pan to accommodate all the fish in one layer, or use 2 pans. Season the fish with salt and pepper. Heat the butter and oil over moderate heat, add the fish and rosemary, and fry about 5-8 minutes each side, or until golden brown and flesh is opaque.

When cooked on both sides, transfer the fish to heated plates. Stir the vinegar and water into the pan, scraping up any browned bits over moderate heat, until the liquid is slightly syrupy. Spoon a little of the pan juices over the fish and serve immediately with a green salad.

Serves 6

173

Fish in crazy water
Pesce all'acqua pazza

Don't be put off by the name; this classic is one of the most versatile and easy dishes to prepare, any season of the year. It's one of my favorite weekend lunches in winter, or Sunday dinners in summer, at the end of a hectic weekend.

You can vary the ingredients endlessly, substituting any other white fish fillets, and add prawns or shrimp or scallops, if you're feeling flush. The one constant is the water, which is boiled with just enough oil to achieve a slight emulsion. After that, you can add almost anything you like.

3½ cups water
3 tablespoons extra virgin olive oil
1 pound black mussels
1 pound clams (vongole)
1 pound fillet of white fish, such as cod or snapper, cut into 4 even pieces
1 large ripe tomato, peeled and coarsely chopped
½ cup dry white wine
3 tablespoons chopped flat-leaf parsley
4 cloves garlic, finely chopped
¼ teaspoon chili flakes
toasted rustic bread, to serve

Combine the water and oil in a pot, bring to a boil and continue boiling for 1 minute. Add the mussels, clams, fish, tomato, wine, parsley, garlic and chili flakes and season with salt and pepper. Bring to a boil, cover the pan and simmer over low heat for 12-15 minutes.

Remove the fish fillet from the pot and place in deep, heated plates. If all the mussels and clams are not open yet, cook these a little longer over high heat. Discard any that have not opened after extra time. Spoon the shellfish and the liquid over the fish and serve immediately with toast on the side. Alternatively, you can place the toast in the plates first, before ladling over the fish and broth.

Serves 4

Fish fillets baked with lemon and oregano
Pesce in teglia al limone e oregano

Despite the utter simplicity, or maybe exactly because of it, this recipe has become a very firm favorite in our house. We enjoy making it with snapper and ruby emperor, but probably most of all with cod, which cooks into beautiful, large, moist flakes. It's great with boiled waxy potatoes, such as fingerling or red potatoes.

¼ cup extra virgin olive oil
¼ cup freshly squeezed lemon juice
1½ tablespoons chopped fresh oregano leaves
1½ tablespoons chopped flat-leaf parsley leaves
4 fish fillets with skin on, such as cod or snapper

Combine the oil, lemon juice, oregano and parsley in a baking dish in which the fillets fit without overlapping. Season the mixture with salt and pepper and whisk to slightly thicken.

Add the fillets, skin side down and spoon the oil and herb mixture over the fish. Let stand 30 minutes or longer at room temperature, turning the fish from time to time.

Meanwhile, preheat the oven to 425°F. Make sure the fish is skin-side down, and season the top with a little more salt and pepper. Bake 10-15 minutes, depending on thickness of the fish. The fish is cooked when it flakes easily when a sharp knife is inserted in the thickest part, and the flesh looks opaque. Serve in deep, heated plates, spoon the sauce over and serve immediately.

Serves 4

Apulian mussel, potato and tomato gratin
Tiella di cozze

The Apulian tiella *is related to the Spanish* paella, *a legacy of the Spanish occupation in the 1600s of the city of Bari in Apulia. It's a versatile oven-baked dish made up of different layers of fish, meat or poultry and vegetables with rice and/or potatoes. An Apulian* tiella *is always made with potatoes – since this is prime potato country – just as a Spanish* paella *is always made with rice.*

Great to serve when people are coming over, as you can put the whole dish together ahead of time, refrigerate, and pop it in the oven about half an hour before serving. Allow a little extra time in the oven if refrigerated. Serve with a crisp green salad.

2 pounds red potatoes, unpeeled
⅓ cup extra virgin olive oil, plus 1½ tablespoons extra
⅓ cup freshly grated parmesan cheese
4 large cloves garlic, finely chopped
½ cup chopped flat-leaf parsley
grated zest of 1 lemon
3 pounds black mussels, beards removed and scrubbed, if necessary
1 pound ripe tomatoes, peeled, seeded and coarsely chopped
1 cup fluffy breadcrumbs (see page 273)

Preheat oven to 375°F.

Cook the potatoes in their skin in salted, boiling water until tender, about 25-30 minutes.

Meanwhile, combine ⅓ cup oil, parmesan, garlic, parsley and lemon zest in a bowl and whisk to combine. Season with salt and pepper and set aside.

Place the mussels in a pot and set over high heat. Cover the pot and cook until all the mussels have opened, about 6 minutes. Shake the pot from time to time. Remove the mussels from the shell, add to the reserved oil mixture and toss well. If the mussels are large, cut them in half lengthwise.

When the potatoes are tender, drain, and when cool enough to handle, remove the skin and slice thickly, to cover the bottom of an oiled gratin dish. Don't worry if the potatoes break up a little, but use the whole batch in one layer. Season with salt and pepper. Spread the mussels in their oil mixture on top and scatter with the tomatoes.

Toss the breadcrumbs in a bowl with the extra 1½ tablespoons oil, until well coated. Scatter over the tomatoes and bake 25 minutes, or until the top is golden and crisp. Let stand a few minutes before serving in deep, heated plates.

Serves 4

Salt cod with chickpeas and gremolata
Baccalà con ceci e gremolata

To be honest, I've never had a good result with real salt cod (baccalà). No matter how long I've soaked and rinsed the fish, the result has always been unpleasantly fishy and salty for my taste. I love the following version, the mild saltiness of the fish alleviated by the perky addition of gremolata *and chickpeas.*

Fish
four cod fillets, about 6 ounces each, with skin on
1½ tablespoons Maldon sea salt
1 teaspoon coarsely ground black pepper
1 teaspoon sugar
1½ tablespoons extra virgin olive oil

Chickpeas
1 pound chickpeas, soaked overnight (see page 108)
2 cups chicken stock or light meat broth (see page 223)

Gremolata
good handful flat-leaf parsley leaves
1 large clove garlic, peeled
good pinch of fresh rosemary leaves
thinly peeled zest of 1 lemon

Sprinkle fish with salt, pepper and sugar. Toss well and refrigerate 4 hours or overnight.

Drain and rinse the chickpeas, and put in a large pan. Add plenty of cold water and season with salt. Cover with a lid and bring to a simmer over very low heat, then simmer, covered partially, until the chickpeas are tender, from 30 minutes to 2 hours, depending on age. Leave to cool in their liquid.

Heat the stock in a large pan and add an equal amount of the chickpea liquor. Drain the chickpeas and add to the stock mixture. Season and heat through.

To make the gremolata, combine the parsley, garlic, rosemary and lemon zest on a board and chop with a chef's knife. Set aside.

Rinse the fish very well, dry on paper towels and season with plenty of pepper. Heat a nonstick frying pan over high heat. Add oil to the pan and cook the fish, skin side down, for 5 minutes or until the skin is crisp, turn and cook 3 minutes on the other side.

Ladle chickpeas with stock into heated plates, place fish on top and scatter with gremolata.

Serves 4

Skate with capers and lemon
Razza con caperi e limone

The Italian version of a French bistro classic. Whereas in France this is prepared in butter (lots of it), cooked until hazelnut brown (beurre noisette), this Italian skate recipe is served with just a little, light lemony sauce – fabulous!

Often skate wings are very large and become too unwieldy for the frying pan (and your plate, for that matter). Try to get nice, small skate wings. Wait until you see the right size and shelve any other plans you may have had for dinner – and eat like a king on a pauper's wage.

4 skate wings, about 6 ounces each
all-purpose flour, for dusting
¼ cup extra virgin olive oil
2 large cloves garlic, bruised with the flat side of a chef's knife
freshly squeezed juice of 1 large lemon
1-2 tablespoons capers, drained, rinsed and drained again, chopped if large
¼ cup chopped flat-leaf parsley leaves

Bring a large frying pan of salted water to a boil. Add the skate in batches and blanch 1-2 minutes. Place the skate in a sinkful of water to cool quickly, then drain and dry, and scrape off the skin with a small knife. Season on both sides with salt and pepper. Place flour in a deep plate, add the skate wings one by one and turn in the flour. Shake off excess.

Heat the oil in a large frying pan over moderately high heat, add the garlic and when it starts to color, add the skate. Cook until brown on the underside, about 4 minutes, then turn over and cook until the other side is golden brown, about another 3-4 minutes.

Add the lemon juice and ½ cup water to the pan and scatter the capers over the wings. Cook another 2 minutes, scraping the pan and letting the liquid bubble up until slightly syrupy, then sprinkle with parsley and serve immediately on heated plates, with pan juices spooned over.

Serves 4

Clams, celery and bean stew
Zuppa di fagioli e vongole

Crisp, herby celery shines in this pastel clams and creamy-white bean dish, making it hearty and light at the same time. I like to heap the clams, celery and cannellini in the middle of a deep, white plate, letting the juices form a pale green moat around them. Go easy on the salt, the clams are quite salty enough by themselves. A squirt of lemon juice provides a light touch.

1½ cups dried cannellini or great northern beans, soaked overnight (see page 108)
¼ cup extra virgin olive oil
4 large cloves garlic, chopped
2 whole stalks celery with leaves, stalks cut into pea-sized cubes, leaves chopped
1 hot red chili, sliced (optional)
3 pounds clams (vongole)
⅓ cup coarsely chopped flat-leaf parsley
crusty bread, to serve
lemon wedges, to serve

Place the soaked beans in a pan and cover with plenty of cold water. Season lightly with salt, cover with a lid and place over low heat. Bring very slowly to a boil, then set the lid at an angle and simmer until the beans are tender, about 30-40 minutes. Set aside in the cooking liquid.

Combine the oil, garlic, celery stalks and chili in a large pan and cook over low heat for 5-10 minutes, without coloring the garlic. Add the clams, place the lid on the pan and cook over moderately high heat until all the shells have opened, about 4 minutes.

Add the beans with 1½ cups of their cooking liquid, and sprinkle with parsley and chopped celery leaves. Replace the lid on the pan and cook over moderate heat for another 5 minutes to heat through. Serve in deep, heated plates, with crusty bread to mop up the juices, and lemon wedges.

Serves 4

Swordfish rolls with salmoriglio
Involtini di pesce spada

Involtini are little rolled up bundles of meat, poultry, fish or vegetables with a savoury stuffing. Salmoriglio is a fabulous Sicilian sauce, used both in cooking, and also to spoon over fish, especially swordfish, or vegetables, such as grilled eggplant, after cooking. It has to be very lemony, herby and garlicky.

1 pound swordfish steaks (about ¾-inch thick)
1½ tablespoons extra virgin olive oil
1 small red onion, halved and thinly sliced
1 large clove garlic, chopped
3 tablespoons chopped basil
3 tablespoons chopped flat-leaf parsley
1¼ cups toasted fluffy breadcrumbs (see page 273)
½ tablespoon capers, drained, chopped

¼ cup provolone piccante cheese, cut into pea-sized cubes
1 large egg, lightly beaten
good pinch chili flakes

Salmoriglio
½ cup extra virgin olive oil
3 tablespoons hot water
freshly squeezed juice of 1 lemon
1½ tablespoons chopped flat-leaf parsley
1½ tablespoons chopped fresh oregano
1 small clove garlic, finely chopped

To make the salmoriglio, pour the oil in a bowl and whisk in the hot water and lemon juice. Add the parsley and oregano, whisking constantly, and then the garlic, until the mixture has thickened. Season with salt.

Cut the skin off the swordfish, then cut the fish into 2 even pieces. Cut these in half horizontally, so you have four thin steaks. Cut the steaks into neat shapes, discarding the bloodlines, setting aside other offcuts for the filling. Place the steaks between 2 sheets of parchment paper and flatten with a smooth mallet until about 6-inch x 4-inch, and uniformly thin. Set aside on a plate.

To make the filling, combine the oil and onion in a frying pan and cook over moderate heat until golden, about 10 minutes, stirring frequently. Stir in the garlic and chopped swordfish offcuts and cook 3 minutes. Add the basil, parsley, toasted breadcrumbs and capers and cook another 2 minutes. Transfer the mixture to a processor and pulse a few times until coarsely chopped. Transfer the mixture to a bowl and stir in the provolone and egg, and season with salt and chili flakes.

Preheat a broiler and place a rack about 4 inches from the heat source.

Spread the filling evenly over the steaks, leaving a ½-inch border all around. Roll up and tie securely with kitchen string. Place the rolls in a baking dish lined with foil and ladle over some of the salmoriglio. Broil 5 minutes each side or until golden, adding a little more salmoriglio when turning to the second side. Serve the involtini in heated, deep plates and pour over the remaining salmoriglio.

Serves 4

In today's congested cities the scooter has made a comeback but it has never been out of fashion in Italy. It's sexy, too – remember "Roman Holiday" and "La Dolce Vita" – and the sound of a Vespa and the sight of a young couple on it is instantly Roman.

Poultry

Chicken with olives and rosemary
Pollo con olive e rosmarino

A typically Roman recipe, redolent of rosemary, flavorful, quick and easy – perfect for a midweek dinner with friends or family. For this chicken recipe, as for any of the others in this book, choose free-range chicken (pollo ruspante).

2 pounds skinless, boneless chicken thighs or breasts, cut into 2-inch pieces
3 tablespoons extra virgin olive oil
1 red onion, halved and thinly sliced
1½ tablespoons chopped fresh rosemary leaves
½ cup dry white wine, or a few tablespoons more, if necessary
½ cup black olives, stoned and chopped
2 anchovy fillets, rinsed and finely chopped
1½ tablespoons red wine vinegar

Dry the chicken on paper towels and transfer to a bowl. Season with salt and pepper and set aside.

Heat the oil over moderately high heat in a sauté pan, add the chicken and brown on all sides, about 5 minutes. Stir in the onion, rosemary and white wine, cover the pan and simmer 10 minutes, turning the chicken a few times.

Stir in the olives and anchovies, crushing the anchovies well into the sauce, and season with plenty of coarsely ground black pepper. Place the lid on the pan and simmer another 10-15 minutes, stirring once or twice, adding a little more wine if the sauce becomes too dry. Stir in the vinegar and serve immediately on a heated platter.

Serves 4-6

Chicken hunter's style
Pollo alla cacciatora

My image of Pollo alla cacciatora *used to be of rather flabby chicken swimming in an insipid tomato, mushroom and bell pepper sauce. That is, until the day we took a little side-trip from Tuscany into Umbria. In an obscure, but highly recommended trattoria in Perugia we ordered the special of the day – you guessed it – Pollo alla cacciatora. A revelation.*

4 pounds free-range chicken thighs, (about 6-8), skin on, bone in
3 tablespoons extra virgin olive oil
2 ounces pancetta, coarsely chopped
½ large onion, coarsely chopped
2 teaspoons coarsely chopped rosemary
4 large cloves garlic, coarsely chopped
1 cup dry white wine
1½ tablespoons red wine vinegar
1½ tablespoons capers, chopped if large
two ¼-inch-thick lemon slices, seeds removed, flesh and peel cut into pea-sized cubes
¼ teaspoon chili flakes
½ cup tangy green olives, pitted and chopped

Choose a pan which can hold all the chicken pieces in one layer, without crowding. Warm the oil over moderately high heat. When hot, add the chicken pieces, skin side down (if the pan is not large enough, do this in two batches). Brown the chicken on both sides, about 10-15 minutes. Transfer to a large plate and season with salt and pepper.

Combine the pancetta, onion, rosemary and garlic in a small processor and pulse until finely chopped. Drain all but 3 tablespoons of the fat from the pan. Add pancetta mixture and sauté over moderate heat for 5 minutes.

Add the wine, vinegar, capers, lemon and chili flakes. Bring to a boil, scraping any browned pieces from the bottom. Return the chicken, with any juices accumulated on the plate, to the pan and stir in the olives. Cover with a lid set at a slight angle and cook over low heat until chicken is tender, about 25 minutes. The chicken is cooked when the juices run clear, and not pink, when a thigh is pierced with a skewer. Add a few tablespoons of water if the pan becomes dry. Transfer the chicken to a warmed platter and pour over the sauce. If the sauce is thin, briefly reduce over high heat.

Serves 6

Chicken with tomato and chili
Pollo all'arrabbiata

Arrabbiata *means "angry" or "in a rage" but in the kitchen it refers to Italian dishes that are cooked in a tomato sauce with hot chilies. The pasta dish* Penne all'arrabbiata *is popular all over Italy.*

¼ cup extra virgin olive oil
1 red onion, cut into 8 wedges
4 whole chicken legs (thighs and legs), about 3 pounds
1 garlic bulb, cloves peeled
½ cup plus 2 tablespoons dry red wine
2 hot red chilies, chopped
1 pint cherry tomatoes, or two 14-ounce cans Italian cherry tomatoes, well drained
polenta, to serve (see page 86)

Soffrito
2 large cloves garlic, peeled and coarsely chopped
2 ounces fatty pancetta, cut into cubes
1 teaspoon fresh rosemary leaves

To make the soffrito, combine the garlic, pancetta and rosemary in a small processor and pulse until fairly finely chopped. Alternatively, this may be done with a sharp cook's knife on a board.

Transfer the mixture to a heavy-based pot, add the oil and cook over moderate heat until the pancetta is golden, about 5 minutes, stirring frequently. Turn heat up to high, add the onion, chicken and garlic cloves and brown the chicken pieces well on both sides, about 8 minutes. Stir in the wine and cook 1 minute, then add chili and tomatoes, and season with salt.

Bring to a simmer, cover with a lid and cook gently for 40 minutes. The chicken is cooked when the liquid runs clear when a skewer is inserted between the thigh and leg. Check seasoning. Serve in deep, heated plates with polenta.

Serves 4

Pan-fried quails with grappa and juniper
Quaglie con grappa e ginepro

Quails are well-liked game meat in Italy, from the north in Piemonte right down to the very south of Sicily. These small birds are most often served on a piece of fried bread, or on polenta or risotto.

12 sage leaves
24 juniper berries, slightly crushed, plus 1 teaspoon juniper berries, slightly crushed
12 quails, washed and dried
12 slices pancetta
3 tablespoons extra virgin olive oil
¼ cup grappa or gin
½ cup dry white wine

Place a sage leaf and 2 juniper berries inside the cavity of each quail. Wrap each quail in a slice of pancetta. Tie securely with kitchen string, tying the legs together as you do so.

Heat a large frying pan over moderately high heat. Add the oil and when hot, but not smoking, add the quails and cook until brown all over, about 8 minutes. Season with salt and pepper. Add the grappa and cook until evaporated. Remove the quails to a heated platter and keep warm.

Add 1 teaspoon crushed juniper berries to the pan, with the wine, and cook, scraping any browned bits from the bottom of the pan, until the liquid is syrupy. Pour over the quails and serve immediately.

Serves 6

Chicken baked with lemon
Pollo al forno con limone

I've lost count of the number of times I've cooked this – both in my classes and for the family – everyone always loves it. The secret is in the aromatic salt, a jar of which is always in my refrigerator. It gives everything, including meat, fish and vegetables, an instant Italian flavor. Please don't repeat the mistake some people in the classes made when they used all the salt in one go – just a teaspoon is enough!

Cooking salt, which is much coarser than table salt, is used to make this aromatic flavoring. The larger salt grains don't dissolve so easily. It keeps up to 3 months.

6 chicken thighs, bone in, skin on
1 lemon, thinly sliced, plus 1 lemon squeezed
1½ tablespoons extra virgin olive oil
⅓ cup water

Aromatic salt
3 cloves garlic, peeled
1 cup cooking salt (coarse salt)
zest of 2 lemons, finely chopped
1½ tablespoons finely chopped fresh rosemary leaves
½ teaspoon freshly ground black pepper
1 bay leaf

To make the aromatic salt, finely chop 2 of the garlic cloves, and reserve the other. Place all ingredients, except the 1 reserved garlic clove and the bay leaves, in a processor and pulse just until the salt is slightly ground. Store mixture in an airtight jar, bury the reserved garlic clove and bay leaf in the salt mixture and refrigerate.

Season the chicken with the aromatic salt, arrange on a plate and cover with plastic wrap. Refrigerate for 2 hours, or overnight.

Preheat the oven to 425°F. Place the sliced lemon in an ovenproof dish. Heat a non-stick pan over moderately high heat. Add the oil and immediately thereafter the chicken, skin side down. Brown well on both sides, about 6 minutes. Arrange the chicken over the lemon slices in the ovenproof dish, skin side up.

Add the lemon juice with the water to the pan in which the chicken was cooked and boil until reduced to a coating consistency, scraping up any browned bits, about 4 minutes. Pour over the chicken in the baking dish. Place the dish in the oven and bake 15-20 minutes, or until the chicken is tender and the juices are no longer pink when pierced. Place on a heated platter, cover loosely with foil and let stand 5 minutes before serving.

Serves 4-6

When Italians get together, it's a sure bet that the talk will turn to food: the relative merits, perhaps, of the "best" chickens from the Arno Valley in Tuscany. Or could it be Nonna's Pollo alla cacciatora of 70 years ago ... or what Mamma is cooking for dinner tonight?

Cornish hens grilled under a brick
Galletto al mattone

Scour streets and building sites for a couple of house bricks, then wrap them in foil. When placed on Cornish hens or chicken, the bricks very effectively keep them pressed flat on the grilling surface, giving an unbelievably crisp skin (you can also use this method on the barbecue). If you don't have a brick, a cast-iron pan, bottom covered with foil, will do the trick.

two 1-1½ pounds Cornish hens
3 tablespoons extra virgin olive oil
small handful thyme sprigs

Preheat a cast iron grill pan and cover two house bricks with foil.

Cut out the backbone of the Cornish hens and open up flat on a cutting board, pressing down well with your hands to flatten the Cornish hen completely. Cut off the wing tips. Brush both sides with oil, season well with salt and pepper and scatter with thyme.

Place the Cornish hens skin side down on the grill pan, put the bricks on top, and cook until the skin is golden brown, about 10 minutes. Turn over, replace the bricks, and cook the other side until just cooked through and the juices run clear when a thigh is pierced, about another 10 minutes, depending on size. Serve with a green salad.

Serves 2

Chicken wrapped in pancetta
Involtini di pollo

Probably the best and most exciting butcher shop I've ever visited was on the beautiful piazza at Greve in Chianti. A huge, hairy boar's head hanging outside the shop announced the fact that selling meat was their business and, once inside, the senses were assaulted by the most wonderful smells, part smoky and part aged meat – huge slabs of fresh (but aged) meats, cured meats, poultry, game, salamis and sausages in all shapes and sizes – and these little involtini. *We bought some and cooked them that night, but they are just as easy to put together yourself. Serve with roast potatoes.*

8 skinless, boneless chicken thigh fillets
2 large cloves garlic, finely chopped
3 tablespoons chopped rosemary leaves
8 slices pancetta
3 tablespoons extra virgin olive oil
½ cup dry white wine

Lay the chicken flat on a surface, smooth side down. Sprinkle with the garlic and rosemary, and season very lightly with salt and pepper. Roll up, drape a slice of pancetta over each, and tie securely with kitchen string. These are the *involtini*.

Heat the oil in a large pan, add the *involtini* and brown over moderate heat on all sides, about 10-15 minutes. Add wine, bring to a simmer, cover the pan and cook gently for 20-30 minutes. Remove the *involtini* to a heated platter and remove string. Boil the cooking juices over high heat until slightly thickened and syrupy. If not enough liquid is left, add water to make a light, syrupy sauce. Serve the chicken on heated plates and spoon over the sauce.

Serves 4

Cornish hens with red wine vinegar
Galletto con aceto di vino rosso

Spatchcock is another term for Cornish hens, and spatchcocking is the method of removing the backbone, and then flattening poultry. Cut with special poultry scissors, or with a sharp knife, on one side of the backbone. Cut on the other side of the backbone, then discard the backbone. Lay the Cornish hen (or chicken) on a board, skin side up, and lean on the bird heavily with the flat of your hand, until you hear a sharp crack. Now the bird is flat and will cook more evenly and much faster.

4 Cornish hens, spatchcocked (see above)
3 tablespoons unsalted butter
1½ tablespoons extra virgin olive oil
1 garlic bulb, cloves separated and peeled
handful thyme sprigs
handful flat-leaf parsley, chopped
½ cup plus 1½ tablespoons red wine vinegar
1 cup chicken stock or broth (see page 223)

Season the Cornish hens inside and out with salt and pepper. Combine the butter and oil in a large, heavy-based frying pan and brown the Cornish hens over moderate heat on both sides. Add garlic and stir until browned, taking care not to burn. Scatter with herbs, cover the pan and simmer over low heat for 20 minutes or until the Cornish hens are cooked through. Remove from the pan and keep warm in a 200°F oven.

Add vinegar to the pan, turn up the heat and scrape up any browned pieces from the bottom. Add stock and cook until the sauce has reduced by half, stirring constantly. Check seasoning. Place the Cornish hens on heated plates and spoon the sauce over.

Serves 4

Rabbit with porcini
Coniglio con porcini

*As I have never been a fan of wild rabbit, finding farmed "white" rabbit was
a revelation. Wild rabbit tends to be tough and takes forever to cook to tenderness,
whereas farmed white rabbit is appreciably larger, giving a more generous meat-to-
bone ratio. I like to marinate this rabbit for at least 48 hours for best flavor.*

½ cup dried porcini mushrooms, soaked in warm water for 20 minutes
1 farmed white rabbit, about 3 pounds, cut into 6-8 pieces (ask the butcher to do this)
all-purpose flour on a plate
3 tablespoons extra virgin olive oil
1 cup veal or chicken stock or broth (see page 223)

Marinade
3 tablespoons red wine vinegar
1 bottle red wine, preferably Chianti
2 large cloves garlic, bruised with the flat side of a chef's knife
1 onion, sliced
1 sprig rosemary
1 large piece lemon peel

For the marinade, combine all ingredients in a bowl, add the rabbit pieces and mix well. Cover
with plastic wrap and refrigerate overnight or longer, turning the pieces a few times, if possible.

For the porcini, line a sieve with a wet paper towel, set over a bowl and pour in the porcini
with liquid. Reserve the porcini liquid for another use, such as risotto or soup. Check the
porcini pieces for grit. Chop coarsely and set aside.

Preheat oven to 275°F. Remove the rabbit from the marinade and dry well on paper towels.
Drain the marinade through a sieve, reserving the liquid and solids separately. Chop the
solids. Season the rabbit pieces with salt and pepper, and dredge in the flour, shaking off any
excess. Heat the oil in a pan, large enough to hold the rabbit in one layer; add the rabbit
pieces and brown well on all sides. Remove to a plate.

Pour the reserved marinade liquid into the pan and bring to a boil, scraping up any browned
bits from the bottom. Add the stock, the rabbit pieces with any accumulated juices, the
reserved porcini and the chopped marinade solids, and bring to a simmer. Cover with
crumpled wet parchment paper, then with a well-fitting lid and bake until the rabbit is tender,
about 2½-3 hours.

Serve the rabbit in deep, heated plates, on a mound of polenta or mashed potatoes, with
plenty of the cooking juices.

Serves 4

Meat & Offal

Pork roast in red wine with juniper berries
Maiale al ginepro

Boston butt roast is a much overlooked cut of pork. With slow, gentle cooking, this inexpensive part of the pig is coaxed into revealing its succulence. Red wine and juniper berries complete the picture. If you have trouble finding juniper berries, you can substitute one teaspoon gin for every two berries (six teaspoons in this recipe). Great for a dinner at home with friends.

4 pounds pork butt roast, tied into a neat cylinder with kitchen string
3 tablespoons extra virgin olive oil
1 bottle full-bodied red wine, such as Shiraz
4 large cloves garlic, bruised with the side of a chef's knife
12 juniper berries, bruised with the side of a chef's knife
2 bay leaves

Choose a heavy-based pot in which the pork fits neatly, with not much room to spare, and with a well-fitting lid. Set over high heat and when hot, add the oil. Swirl it around to coat the bottom and most of the sides of the pan. Add the pork and brown it on all sides, about 10-15 minutes. Season with salt and pepper as you turn the roast.

Add the wine – it should almost reach the top of the pork, if not, add a little more. Add the garlic, juniper berries and bay leaves and bring to a simmer. Cover the pot with wet, crumpled parchment paper or aluminium foil and simmer over very low heat for 3-4 hours, or until the pork is very tender. Turn the meat from time to time.

Remove pork to a plate, tent loosely with foil and let stand 10-20 minutes. If the cooking liquid in the pan is thin, return to a high heat and reduce until it coats the back of a spoon.

Slice the pork and arrange on a heated platter. Pour over some of the pan juices and pour the remaining sauce in a sauceboat to serve at the table.

Serves 6-8

Cabbage rolls in tomato sauce
Valigiette (suitcases)

Hungary is not the only country to lay claim to cabbage rolls – they are a specialty in Milan, where they're mostly stuffed with veal. Everywhere in the northern regions of Italy stuffed cabbage rolls can be found, such as rambasici *in Liguria and Friuli.*

1 whole savoy cabbage
¾ pound ground pork
6 ounces pancetta, finely chopped
1 large clove garlic, finely chopped
3 tablespoons chopped flat-leaf parsley
½ cup fresh breadcrumbs
⅔ cup freshly grated parmesan cheese
1 large egg, lightly beaten
⅓ cup extra virgin olive oil
½ cup dry white wine, plus ½ cup extra
14-ounce can Italian cherry tomatoes, with juice
good pinch chili flakes (optional)

Detach the leaves from the cabbage. From a large cabbage, you need about 6-8 large, unbroken leaves, or 12-14 whole leaves from a small cabbage. Bring a large pot of lightly salted water to a boil and blanch the leaves for 1-2 minutes, or until they are pliable enough to fold around the meat later. It's easiest not to cook all the leaves at once, maybe just 1 or 2 at a time. Remove from the pot and set aside in a large colander or bowl.

Combine the pork, pancetta, garlic, parsley, breadcrumbs, parmesan and egg in a large bowl and mix with your hands until the mixture is smooth. Shape into 12 even sausage shapes (about 3 inches each).

Place a whole cabbage leaf on a board. For larger leaves, cut out the center spine to halve. Place a meat portion on the leaf and roll up, folding in the sides. When all the leaves and filling have been used, squeeze each bundle very firmly between two hands, to remove any excess moisture and to make the cabbage adhere to the meat.

Heat the oil over moderately high heat in a pan which can accommodate the rolls in one layer. When the oil is hot, add the rolls and cook until browned on all sides, about 20 minutes. Add half the wine, set the lid at an angle, and simmer over moderate heat until most of the wine has evaporated, about 20 minutes. Add the remaining wine and the tomatoes with their juice and chili flakes, and simmer another 20 minutes. Let stand a few minutes before serving.

Serves 4-6

Roast spareribs with apples
Puntine con le mele

A refreshing departure from American-style ribs. If you have the time, do take the trouble to marinate the pork with the flavorings overnight in the refrigerator. The garlic and rosemary impregnate the ribs more effectively over a long period, and doing this the night before cuts down on preparation the next day. I like to serve this with mashed potatoes.

3 tablespoons chopped fresh rosemary
4 large cloves garlic, chopped
1 teaspoon extra virgin olive oil, plus extra for the apples
4 pounds pork spareribs, each about 1½-inch thick
6 small apples, halved

Combine the rosemary, garlic and oil in a small bowl. Rub all over the ribs, place them in a dish and cover with plastic wrap. Refrigerate overnight.

Preheat the oven to 325°F. Line a large baking dish with foil. Season the ribs well on all sides with salt and pepper, then place them in one layer in the prepared dish, tucking in the apples here and there. Brush the cut surfaces of the apples with a little oil. Roast for 60 minutes, or until the ribs and the apples are golden and tender.

Preheat the broiler.

Set the pan with the ribs about 6 to 8 inches from the heat and cook them until golden brown and crisp on all sides, about 15 minutes each side, turning them occasionally. Remove the apples when they become tender, about halfway through broiling, and keep them warm. When the spareribs are cooked, serve them with the apples on heated plates.

Serves 6

Meat essence
Sugo di carne

I would never be without this in my freezer. There's hardly a dish which is not improved by these concentrated meat juices – sugo di carne (meat essence) will lift any dish out of the ordinary, and turn a good dish into something sublime. Stir into a risotto, pasta or a stew. Think of it as an instant flavor and texture boost.

Normally I freeze the juices in 1-cup round containers, not filling them right to the top. When ready to use, defrost a container partially, just long enough to cut into it with a sharp knife, and divide the contents into 4 equal wedges. Use what's needed and refreeze the rest. (Some people may have reservations about refreezing something which has been partially defrosted, however I have done this for years without ill effect, so you'll have to make up your own mind about that.)

Don't forget about the type of *sugo* that manifests "naturally," such as the sticky, meaty residue in a roasting dish, or the gelatinous juices left after making dishes such as schinco (page 238) or ossobuco (page 242). Never discard these precious juices; instead freeze them until needed.

To extract maximum gelatine, it's important to use meat and chicken on the bone.

If you need meat essence in a hurry and there's none in your freezer, you can always resort to the excellent veal glace most good butchers sell. It's not the same, but as a flavor boost it works.

¼ cup extra virgin olive oil
2 ounces pancetta, chopped
2 ounces prosciutto, chopped
1 large onion, sliced
1 medium carrot, sliced
1 stalk celery with leaves, sliced
1 pound chicken wings
1 pound meaty veal bones, such as shanks, any fat trimmed
2 pounds meaty beef bones, such as beef ossobuco, any fat trimmed
1 bay leaf
4 cloves
1 cup dry red wine
14 cups stock, chicken, veal, beef or a mixture, preferably homemade, or broth (see page 223)
14-ounce can diced tomatoes, well drained
2 cloves garlic, bruised with the flat blade of a chef's knife

Combine the oil, pancetta and prosciutto in a very large pan and top with the onions, carrot, celery, chicken, veal and beef. If your pan is not large enough, divide the mixture among two pans and cook simultaneously.

(Continued next page)

Meat essence

(Continued from previous page)

Set over moderately high heat and cook, without stirring, in an uncovered pan, until you can smell the onion and the mixture is sizzling, about 10 minutes.

Turn the pieces of meat to brown on all sides, about 20 minutes. Stir in the bay leaf and the cloves, then pour in the wine. Simmer gently, scraping up any browned bits from the bottom, until wine has completely reduced, about 8 minutes. Add 2 cups of the stock and simmer until liquid has reduced to a brown glaze, about 20 minutes. Repeat adding 2 cups of the stock twice, each time simmering 20 minutes or until only a thick brown glaze remains in the bottom of the pot.

Stir in the remaining 8 cups stock, together with the tomatoes and garlic. Simmer gently, with the lid at an angle, for 6 hours. Make sure the meat stays nearly submerged with stock. If not, add a little more stock or hot water.

Set a large colander over a large bowl, turn the contents of the pan into the colander and press down hard on the solids. Discard the solids. Cool the meat essence, then cover with plastic wrap and refrigerate overnight. The next day, remove any solidified fat from the surface and slightly warm the mixture to liquefy. Transfer to smaller containers and freeze for up to 6 months.

Makes about 4 cups

Broth

Italians like to use broth (brodo) made from a variety of meaty bones and vegetables. Veal bones, and chicken wings and necks give good body, containing plenty of gelatin. Tell your butcher you're making stock – he may have some nice bones tucked away in that mysterious area behind the shop.

These light broths are suitable for risottos, soups and stews. Don't over-salt them, as they may have to be reduced at some later stage. Any broth left over may be brought back to a boil, and refrozen in smaller containers.

a quantity of veal bones (if possible with some meat attached) – if veal bones are not available, substitute with
  beef bones, (not pork or lamb) or use only chicken
a quantity of chicken bones (carcass, wings and necks)
1 large red onion, unpeeled, cut in half
1 whole garlic bulb, unpeeled, cut in half horizontally
4 stalks celery, cut into large pieces
handful flat-leaf parsley with stalks
good splash white wine
½-1 teaspoon salt and a small handful black peppercorns

Combine the meat and chicken bones in a large pot and add the onion, garlic, celery, parsley, wine and salt and pepper. Fill the pot with water up to 1 inch from the top and bring to a simmer. Skim scum off the top from time to time. Once simmering steadily, set the lid at an angle and simmer very gently for anything up to 6 hours, but at least 2 hours, with just the occasional bubble breaking the surface. The broth will become more flavorful with longer cooking.

Strain the stock through a colander into a large bowl (or several bowls) and place in the refrigerator overnight. Next morning scrape any solidified fat from the top. Warm the congealed stock slightly and pour through a fine sieve into suitable freezer containers. I usually use 4 cups capacity rectangular containers, which stack neatly in the freezer.

Slow-cooked beef cheeks
Guancia di manzo

There's nothing like the velvety quality beef cheeks develop with long, slow cooking. You may have to order these from your butcher, or they may be available frozen in packets of 6. Serve with polenta.

6 beef cheeks, about 3 pounds
¼ cup extra virgin olive oil
2 large red onions, chopped
1 carrot, cut into ¼-inch rounds
2 stalks celery, cut into ¼-inch pieces
¼ pound pancetta, cut into pea-sized cubes
2 cups full-bodied red wine, such as Shiraz
2 cups tomato sauce (see page 26)
soft polenta, to serve (see page 86)

Season the beef cheeks well with salt and pepper. Heat the oil over high heat in a large, heavy pot, and when just starting to smoke, add the beef cheeks and cook until browned on both sides, about 10 minutes. Transfer to a plate.

Pour any excess oil from the pot, leaving about 3 tablespoons. Add the onions, carrot, celery and pancetta and cook over moderate heat until vegetables have softened, about 8 minutes, stirring frequently. Add the wine and tomato sauce and bring to a boil.

Add the beef cheeks and bring to a simmer over very low heat. Place a piece of wet, crumpled parchment paper over the top of the pot, close the lid securely over the paper and cook until the beef is very tender, about 3-4 hours. Serve in deep, heated plates.

Serves 6

Tuscan meatloaf
Polpettone alla Toscana

Polpettone is meatloaf, and polpette are meatballs. We recently cooked this meatloaf in my classes and most people were amazed at how good it was. Giving the meatloaf the real Tuscan treatment of a good crust before baking makes all the difference: an appetizing roast-like appearance.

The sauce, which is no more than canned tomatoes, baked along with the meat, takes on the delicious meaty flavors. Serve with a green salad.

2 thick slices Italian-type bread, such as *pane di casa* or ciabatta, crusts removed, bread
  torn into large pieces and soaked in milk to cover
1 pound lean ground beef
1 pound ground pork or veal
¼ pound prosciutto or pancetta, chopped
½ cup parmesan cheese, freshly grated
¼ cup chopped flat-leaf parsley
2 large eggs, lightly beaten
¼ cup extra virgin olive oil
1 cup dry white wine
two 14-ounce cans diced tomatoes, with juice

Squeeze the bread to remove excess milk, crumble and combine in a large bowl with the beef, pork, prosciutto, parmesan, parsley and eggs. Season with salt and pepper and mix well with your hands. Fry a small patty to check seasoning.

Shape the meat into a ball, place on a rimless (or upside-down) lightly oiled baking sheet and compact the meat with your hands, forming it into a loaf shape, about 10-inch x 5-inch. Cover with plastic wrap and refrigerate for at least 1 hour.

Preheat the oven to 325°F. Heat the oil in a roasting dish set over moderately high heat. Slide the meatloaf into the roasting dish and cook, without disturbing, until the bottom is browned and crisp, about 6-8 minutes. Turn over carefully. Add the wine and cook 5 minutes, or until slightly reduced. Add the tomato sauce and cover the meatloaf with parchment paper, pressing it on to the top and sides of the meatloaf. Cover the whole dish with foil and bake 40 minutes. Remove the roasting dish from the oven and let stand 15 minutes.

Transfer the meatloaf to a board and cover loosely with foil. Place the roasting dish over moderate heat, scraping up any browned bits from the bottom and sides of the pan. Cook until the sauce has slightly thickened. Check seasoning. Cut the meatloaf into slices and serve on heated plates with the tomato sauce.

Serves 8

Beef shanks in red wine
Ossobuco di manzo in vino rosso

Beef shanks are similar to veal ossobuco *(lit. hollow bone), but beef has a richer quality, making this a winter dish worthy of using your best red wine for cooking.*

5 pounds slices beef shank, each about 1¼-inch thick
¼ cup extra virgin olive oil
¼ pound pancetta in one piece, cut into pea-sized cubes
2 large onions, chopped
4 large cloves garlic, chopped
3 tablespoons all-purpose flour
4 cups beef or veal stock

Marinade
1 bottle full-bodied red wine, preferably Chianti
3 tablespoons red wine vinegar
1 large onion, thickly sliced
¼ teaspoon chili flakes

Place the beef in a large bowl and cover with the marinade ingredients. Cover with plastic wrap and refrigerate for at least 6 hours, or overnight.

Preheat the oven to 275°F.

Remove the beef from the marinade, but do not discard the marinade. Dry the beef on paper towels. Tie the slices with kitchen string to ensure they won't fall apart while cooking.

Heat oil in a large, heavy-bottomed casserole. Add the pancetta and brown, then remove with a slotted spoon to a plate and set aside. Turn the heat up to high, add the meat and brown on both sides. If the pan is not large enough to contain the meat in one layer, do this in two batches. Remove the beef to a plate and set aside.

Add the onions and stir over moderate heat until golden. Add the garlic and stir 1 minute. Sprinkle with flour and cook 3 minutes, stirring to coat and lightly brown the flour.

Return the beef and pancetta to the pan, cover with the marinade and season with salt and pepper. Add enough stock to just cover the meat, bring to a boil and cover with wet, crumpled parchment paper, and a lid. Bake for 3 hours, checking from time to time if the liquid simmers very gently, just the occasional bubble on the surface. Adjust the oven temperature, if necessary.

Remove the beef to a heated plate and boil the juices until they have thickened to a light coating consistency. Pour the sauce over the beef and serve in deep, heated plates.

Serves 6

Pot roast of beef
Stracotto di manzo al Barolo

It goes without saying that in Piemonte barolo is used to cook this meat, as well as poured at the table. This fabulous wine, made from the Nebbiolo grape, is very expensive elsewhere, so choose a cheaper full-bodied red wine, such as shiraz. Stracotto means "overcooked." Serve with mashed or boiled potatoes.

3 tablespoons extra virgin olive oil, plus 3 tablespoons extra
4 pounds beef, preferably chuck, in one piece, tied into a neat shape
1 onion, chopped
1 celery stalk, chopped
1 small carrot, chopped
2 large cloves garlic, finely chopped
1½ cups full-bodied red wine
1 cup beef, veal or chicken stock, preferably homemade, or broth (see page 223)
1 roma tomato, chopped
few fresh thyme sprigs

Preheat the oven to 275°F. Heat a heavy-based frying pan over high heat, add the oil and when just starting to smoke, add the beef and brown well on all sides. Remove the beef from the pan and set aside on a plate. Don't wash the frying pan.

Combine the extra oil, onion, celery and carrot in a large oven-safe pot and cook over low heat until the vegetables soften, about 10 minutes. Add the garlic and stir 1 minute more. Place the meat with any accumulated juices on the vegetables.

Remove any excess fat from the frying pan, being careful not to remove any of the browned bits. Add the wine to the frying pan and boil over high heat, scraping up any browned bits from the bottom, for about 1 minute only. Pour over the meat in the casserole.

Add stock, tomato and thyme sprigs to the casserole and season with salt and pepper. Bring to a boil over high heat, cover the casserole with wet, crumpled parchment paper and the lid, and transfer to the oven. Cook for 3 hours, basting with the liquid from time to time. Check that the beef is cooking at a very gentle simmer, just the rare bubble breaking the surface. If the liquid simmers too vigorously, turn the heat down. If the liquid evaporates, add a little hot water.

When the meat is tender when tested with a skewer or the tip of a sharp knife, remove it to a board. Reduce the liquid in the pan to obtain a slightly thickened pouring consistency, or if there's not enough liquid in the casserole, add a little stock or water and cook briefly, stirring constantly. Check seasoning. Slice the meat thickly and arrange on a heated platter. Pour over a few tablespoons of the sauce and serve the remainder at the table. Serve immediately with mashed or boiled potatoes.

Serves 6

Oxtails with tomato, white wine and garlic
Coda alla vaccinara

An eternal favorite in Roman trattorias, oxtails cook to complete tenderness, with great flavor, due to the meat cooked "on the bone." The other bonus of cooking on the bone is the fabulous rich sauce that develops. Shred leftover meat and combine with any remaining sauce to make a superb pasta sauce.

3 tablespoons extra virgin olive oil
4 pounds oxtails, trimmed
all-purpose flour on a plate
2 ounces pancetta in one piece
2 large onions, chopped
2 stalks celery with leaves, if available, stalks sliced, leaves chopped and reserved
4 large cloves garlic, bruised with the flat side of a chef's knife
few small rosemary sprigs
4 juniper berries, crushed
1½ cups dry white wine
two 14-ounce cans cherry tomatoes, drained and left whole, or roma tomatoes, drained and
  coarsely chopped
1½ cups stock, either chicken, veal or beef, or a mixture, preferably
  homemade, or broth (see page 223)
1½ tablespoons balsamic vinegar
¼ cup chopped flat-leaf parsley

Preheat oven to 275°F.

Heat the oil over moderately high heat in a heavy-based oven-safe pot with a well-fitting lid. Season the oxtails with salt and pepper, then dredge them in flour, shaking off any excess.

When the oil is hot, but not smoking, brown the oxtails on all sides. Do this in batches if the pan is not large enough. Reduce the heat to moderate and stir in the piece of pancetta, onions, celery, garlic, rosemary sprigs and juniper berries. Sauté for 5 minutes, or until the onions are softening. Add the wine and simmer 5 minutes, then stir in the tomatoes and stock. The meat should be barely covered with the liquid. Bring to a simmer. Cover the pot with crumpled, wet parchment paper, then place the lid securely over the top.

Bake 2½-3 hours, making sure the pot simmers very gently, with just the occasional bubble breaking the surface. Remove the pot from the oven and remove the oxtails carefully from the liquid and keep warm. If the liquid is thin, reduce it briefly over high heat. Stir the balsamic vinegar in the sauce and check seasoning. Return the oxtails to the pot and heat through. Stir in the reserved celery leaves and the parsley. Serve in deep heated plates.

Serves 4

No matter whether you're in the big city or the country, meals on the Italian table are essentially the same. Dishes such as Rigatoni with cabbage and fontina *(page 54)* are just as popular in a smart restaurant as in a farmhouse kitchen after a long day in the fields.

Veal meatballs in lima bean soup
Minestra con polpette di vitello

Curly endive – or any other bitter green such as chicory, radicchio or arugula – gives this soup great flavor, with just a hint of piquancy. The bitterness, which mellows considerably with cooking, is just the right counterbalance to the smooth flavor of the veal and the big, satiny lima beans. Serve with crusty bread.

3 tablespoons extra virgin olive oil
1 large onion, chopped
1 stalk celery, thinly sliced
2 large carrots, sliced
2 large cloves garlic, chopped
6 cups broth (see page 223) or water
1 large head curly endive, tough stems removed, leaves cut into strips
1 cup dried lima beans, cooked (see page 108) and reserved in their liquid

Veal meatballs
2 slices Italian-type bread, crusts removed
½ cup water
1 pound ground veal
1½ tablespoons chopped red onion
1 large egg, lightly beaten
3 tablespoons finely chopped flat-leaf parsley
3 tablespoons extra virgin olive oil

Make the meatballs first: place the bread in a bowl and cover with water. Let stand until the water has been absorbed, about 5 minutes, then squeeze the bread until very dry. Crumble into a bowl, add the veal, onion, egg and parsley and season with salt and pepper. Check seasoning by making a tiny patty and fry so you can taste it. Adjust seasoning, if necessary. Shape the mixture into walnut-sized balls with wet hands. Heat a non-stick frying pan over moderate heat. When the pan is hot, add the oil and when hot but not smoking, add the balls in one layer and cook until browned on all sides. Set aside.

Combine the oil, onion, celery and carrots in a large pan and cook over moderately low heat until the vegetables start to soften, about 10 minutes, stirring frequently. Stir in the garlic and stir 1 minute more. Add the broth, bring to a boil and simmer 10 minutes.

Stir in the endive, the drained beans and the meatballs and simmer another 5 minutes. Serve in heated bowls.

Serves 6

Braised whole veal shanks
Schinco

When the whole shank is cooked, rather than cut into slices as for ossobuco, *it's referred to as "schinco" or "stinco," the latter a source of great merriment when children are at the table.* Schinco or stinco *can be veal, lamb or pork shank, cooked on the bone, with veal* schinco *a specialty of Trieste. This cut is always carved before serving. A veal shank normally serves 2 people, whereas a yearling or pork shank easily feeds 3-4 people. Ask for hind shanks – these are meatier than front ones. Also ask the butcher to cut off the meatless end of the shanks, but take them home: they make fabulous gelatinous stock.*

¼ cup extra virgin olive oil
1 red onion, chopped
3 veal shanks, preferably hind shanks
6 anchovies, drained
4 large cloves garlic, bruised with the flat side of a cook's knife
6 sage leaves
½ cup dry white wine
2 cups homemade stock, preferably veal stock, or broth (see page 223)

Combine the oil and onion in an oven-safe pot, large enough to hold the shanks comfortably, and cook over moderate heat until the onion is soft, about 5 minutes. Turn the heat up to moderately high, add the shanks and brown thoroughly on all sides, about 15 minutes. This may have to be done in batches. Remove the shanks from the pot and keep warm.

Remove any charred onions from the pot. Add the anchovies, garlic and sage to the pot and pour in the wine. Bring to a boil, scraping up any browned bits from the bottom of the pot. Stir in the stock and bring to a simmer. Reduce heat to low, return the veal on their bones to the pot, and cover the pot with a sheet of parchment paper. Place the lid securely on top and simmer 1 hour, making sure the liquid simmers gently, with just the occasional bubble breaking the surface. Alternatively, you can braise the dish in a 275°F oven. Check from time to time and turn temperature down as necessary.

Remove the casserole from the heat and turn the shanks over. Cook another hour, or until the meat is very tender.

Remove the meat on their bones from the pot and cut the meat away from the bones, into large serving pieces. If the liquid is thin, reduce over high heat. Return the liquid to the pot, together with the meat. Reheat for a few minutes, then serve immediately from the pot, in deep, heated plates.

Serves 6

Homemade sausage
Salsiccia di casa

With all the talk today of increasing incidence of food allergies and intolerances, this homemade sausage meat is a wonderful standby. Unlike store-bought sausages, you'll know exactly what went into the mix. Feel free to add other herbs or spices, but keep in mind that a "plainer" mixture will be more adaptable. In this book you'll find numerous ways to use this sausage meat, such as in pastas and soups, but I'm sure you can think of plenty yourself.

¼ teaspoon salt
½ clove garlic
2 teaspoons red wine vinegar
1¾ pounds coarsely ground pork, beef, veal or chicken
3 tablespoons chopped flat-leaf parsley
¼ teaspoon chili flakes (optional)
pinch of ground nutmeg

Combine the salt and garlic in a mortar and crush to a paste. Stir in the red wine vinegar. Place the pork in a bowl, add salt, garlic and vinegar mixture, the parsley, chili flakes, if used, and nutmeg. Mix well with your hands.

Divide the mixture into 5 even parts and roll each into a sausage shape. Wrap securely in plastic wrap, twisting the ends, and refrigerate or freeze.

Recipes in this book using homemade sausage:
• Penne with sausage, pancetta and eggs (page 28)
• Sausage and cranberry bean risotto (page 76)
• Rice cake with provolone and sausage (page 84)
• Polenta with sausage, ham and pancetta (page 90)
• Farro and vegetable soup with pancetta (page 92)

Ossobuco cooked in red wine
Ossobuco in bianco

People often think "in bianco" means food cooked in white wine – in fact, it simply means it's cooked without tomatoes. Gremolata and Risotto alla milanese (see page 68) are traditionally served with ossobuco.

6 large pieces veal ossobuco
all-purpose flour for dusting
3 tablespoons extra virgin olive oil, plus 1½ tablespoons extra
1 large red onion, cut into chunks
4 celery stalks, thinly sliced
4 cloves garlic, crushed, but left in one piece
8 anchovies, drained
½ bottle full-bodied red wine
1 cup good, gelatinous broth (see page 223)

Gremolata
handful flat-leaf parsley
1 large clove garlic, peeled
zest of 2 lemons

Preheat oven to 275°F.

Tie the pieces of ossobuco with kitchen string, then dust the pieces with flour, shaking off any excess. Choose a large oven-safe pot with a well-fitting lid, which can hold all the pieces in one layer. Set the pot over moderately high heat and when hot, add 3 tablespoons of the oil and swirl it around. Add the ossobuco and brown on both sides. Remove from the pot, set aside on a plate and season with salt and pepper.

Add the remaining tablespoon oil, add the onion and celery and cook over moderate heat until soft, about 10 minutes. Add the garlic and anchovies and stir 1 minute. Add the wine, bring to a boil, scraping up any browned bits from the bottom, then stir in the broth.

Return the ossobuco to the pot and bring to a gentle simmer. Cover with crumpled wet parchment paper, then cover with the lid. Bake in the oven for 2½-3 hours, or until the meat is very tender. Check from time to time to make sure the liquid simmers very gently, just the occasional bubble on the surface.

To make the gremolata, chop the ingredients together and combine in a small bowl.

Serve the ossobuco in deep, heated plates, with gremolata sprinkled over. Serve with *Risotto alla milanese* (see page 68) or boiled or mashed potatoes.

Serves 6

Braised veal shoulder with white wine
Vitello brasato al vino bianco

There's no occasion where this wonderful veal braise wouldn't be welcomed with open arms. Whether having colleagues, the in-laws, best friends or the family coming over to dinner, this is always a hit. The secret is very long, slow cooking. The meat will be so tender, you could eat it with a spoon. Like with so many veal dishes, a good accompaniment is cannellini beans.

1 boned veal shoulder (also sold as veal blade)
2 cloves garlic, finely chopped
2 teaspoons chopped rosemary leaves
3 tablespoons extra virgin olive oil
2 ounces pancetta, chopped
1 cup dry white wine
1 cup veal or chicken stock, or broth (see page 223)

Preheat oven to 275°F.

Lay the veal flat on a cutting board, skin side down. Season the inside with pepper and scatter with garlic and rosemary. Rub these in well. Roll the veal up and tie with kitchen string into a neat roll.

Heat the oil over moderately high heat, in an oven-safe pot with a well-fitting lid, in which the veal will fit snugly. Add the veal and brown on all sides, about 15 minutes. Remove veal to a plate.

Add the pancetta to the pot and brown, about 4 minutes, stirring frequently. Add the wine, scraping up any browned bits from the bottom. Add the stock and bring to a boil. Return the veal to the pot, cover the pan with crumpled wet parchment paper and set the lid securely on top. Braise in the oven for 3 hours. Check from time to time if the liquid is simmering slowly, with just the occasional bubble on the surface. Adjust the oven temperature accordingly.

To serve, remove the veal from the pan and keep warm. Set the pan over high heat to reduce the cooking liquid until you have a slight coating consistency. Slice the veal and serve with the pan juices.

Serves 6

Veal bundles with mozzarella and prosciutto
Involtini di vitello

This recipe has been with me so long, it feels like part of the family, and what's more, the whole family loves it. When people come over to dinner, you can have it prepared in advance and even after all these years it always seems quite special. Involtini are little roulades or bundles: they can be made with meat, fish (see Swordfish rolls with salmoriglio, page 186) or even vegetables, such as eggplant. Serve with roast potatoes.

4 veal scallops
3 ounces mozzarella cheese
2 ounces sliced prosciutto
½ cup Italian parsley
⅓ cup freshly grated parmesan cheese
3 tablespoons extra virgin olive oil
½ cup dry white wine

Pound the veal between plastic wrap (or inside a bag) until thin.

Combine mozzarella, prosciutto and parsley on a board and chop together. Combine in a bowl with the parmesan and season with salt and pepper.

Lay the veal flat on a board and divide the mixture between the veal. Roll the veal up, enclosing the filling, and tie securely with kitchen string.

Heat the oil in a heavy-based pan and cook the bundles over moderate heat until golden on all sides. Season lightly, add the wine and cook gently for 10 minutes, or until cooked through and the sauce thickens slightly. Transfer the *involtini* to a heated serving plate and keep warm.

Add a few tablespoons hot water to the pan and over high heat scrape up any browned bits from the bottom and stir until the liquid is syrupy. Remove the string from the *involtini* and drizzle a little of the sauce over them.

Serves 4

Calf's tongue with gherkin and caper dressing
Lingua di vitello con cetriolini e capperi

If the mention of tongue is enough to turn you off, you should definitely try it the Italian way. With this cooking method, the tongue is first simmered until nearly tender, and then slices are pan-fried until golden and crisp. Result: firm texture and wonderful piquancy.

1 calf's tongue, about 1¾ pounds
handful flat-leaf parsley with stalks
1 sprig sage
1 bay leaf
flour, for dusting
¼ cup extra virgin olive oil
⅓ cup plus 1½ tablespoons dry white wine
1 large gherkin or dill pickle, drained and cut into tiny dice
1 heaped tablespoon capers, drained, chopped if large

Place the tongue in a pan and cover with salted water. Add the parsley, sage and bay leaf and bring to a boil. Turn heat down and simmer 60 minutes. Remove from the water and, when cool enough to handle, pull or cut off the skin.

Slice the tongue about ½-inch thick and dust the slices with flour seasoned with salt and pepper. Heat the olive oil over moderately high heat in a frying pan and cook the slices in batches until crisp and golden on both sides, about 5 minutes first side, then 3-4 minutes second side. Drain on paper towels and arrange on a serving dish.

Remove all but 3 tablespoons of the fat from the pan, add the wine, gherkins and capers and warm over low heat. Check seasoning and pour over the tongue. Serve warm or cold. If refrigerating, return to room temperature before serving.

Serves 4

Venetian calf's liver
Fegato alla veneziana

The trick with liver cooked the Italian way is fast and fierce. Serve with garlicky greens, such as chicory or broccoli raab (see page 134).

3 tablespoons extra virgin olive oil
1½ tablespoons unsalted butter, plus 1½ tablespoons extra
1 pound red onions, thinly sliced
1 pound calf's liver, thinly sliced
handful sage leaves
¼ cup Marsala
3 tablespoons red wine
handful flat-leaf parsley, leaves chopped

Heat the oil and 1½ tablespoons butter in a large frying pan. Add the onions and cook over moderate heat for 10-15 minutes, or until very soft.

Meanwhile, pat liver dry on paper towels, and cut into ½-inch strips.

Transfer the onion with a slotted spoon to a heated plate and cover loosely with foil to keep warm. Turn the heat under the frying pan up to high, and when pan is really hot and starting to smoke, add the liver and sage leaves. Season with salt and pepper and sauté 2 minutes, until the liver has browned.

Add Marsala and wine and cook 2 minutes, or until the liquid becomes syrupy. Return the onions to the pan, stir in the remaining 1½ tablespoons butter and the parsley. Cook another 2 minutes to heat through and serve immediately. Serve with greens and creamy mashed potatoes or polenta.

Serves 4

Braised lamb shanks
Cosciotto d'agnello brasato

Is there anyone out there who doesn't like lamb shanks?

6 small lamb shanks, about 10 ounces each
1 bottle red wine
3 large carrots, peeled and cut into bite-sized pieces
3 red onions, peeled and quartered
2 stalks celery, cut into ½-inch pieces
4 large cloves garlic, lightly bruised
8 cloves
5 juniper berries, slightly crushed, or 2½ tablespoons gin
4 bay leaves
1 cinnamon stick
plenty of coarsely ground black pepper
3 tablespoons extra virgin olive oil

Combine the shanks in a large bowl with all the other ingredients, except the oil. Refrigerate overnight, turning the shanks from time to time.

Remove the meat from the marinade and dry well with paper towels. Set aside and reserve the marinade.

Heat the oil over moderate heat in a large, heavy-based pot with a well-fitting lid, in which the shanks fit snugly, without overlapping. Brown the shanks until golden on all sides, about 10-15 minutes. Season with salt and pepper. Remove the shanks to a platter. Pour off the fat from the pot and set the pot aside.

Remove the bay leaves and cinnamon from the marinade and reserve. Strain the marinade through a colander and reserve both the liquid and the solids.

Return the pot to the heat and add the solids. Cook over moderately high heat until just heated through, about 3-4 minutes. Return the shanks, together with the reserved bay leaves and cinnamon. Add the liquid marinade and season with salt and pepper.

Bring to a boil, place a sheet of crumpled wet parchment paper over the top of the pot, then place the lid securely on top. Reduce the heat to a low simmer, just the occasional bubble on the surface, and cook until the shanks are very tender, about 2½-3 hours. Serve the shanks in deep, heated plates, with mashed potatoes or polenta.

Serves 6

Tripe with cacciatori sausage
Tripa con salsicce cacciatori

Both tripe and cacciatori sausages are well liked in Lombardy, and particularly in Milan. Milanese are called "busecconi" (tripe eaters). Serve with a green salad.

3 pounds honeycomb tripe
¼ cup extra virgin olive oil
1½ tablespoons unsalted butter, plus 1½ tablespoons extra
handful flat-leaf parsley, leaves removed and chopped, stalks finely chopped
½ cacciatori sausage (about 3½ ounces), skin removed, chopped
1 small onion, finely chopped
½ pound celery, diced
3 large cloves garlic, bruised with the flat side of a cook's knife
1 teaspoon chopped rosemary leaves
1½ cups dry white wine
14-ounce can Italian peeled roma tomatoes, coarsely chopped, with their juice
2 hot red chilies, chopped
1½ cups meat broth (see page 223)
1¼ cups freshly grated parmesan cheese

Bring a large pot of water to a boil, add salt and the tripe, and simmer 2 hours, or until tender. Drain and cut tripe into ½-inch strips. Set aside.

Combine the oil, 1½ tablespoons butter, chopped parsley stalks and cacciatori in a large, heavy-based pot and cook over moderate heat until the cacciatori has changed color, about 10 minutes. Remove with a slotted spoon to a plate and set aside.

Add the onion to the pot and cook until onion is soft and golden, about 5 minutes, stirring frequently. Add the celery and stir 1 minute. Stir in the garlic, chopped parsley leaves and rosemary, then add the reserved tripe and cook 5 minutes, stirring from time to time.

Add the wine, bring to a simmer and cook 1 minute, then stir in the tomatoes with their juice, the chilies and the reserved cacciatori. Season with salt and pepper and add the broth. Bring to a steady simmer.

Cover the pot with crumpled wet parchment paper and place a lid securely on top. Cook 2-2½ hours or until the tripe is very tender. Alternatively, place the pot in a 275°F oven for the same length of time. Check regularly if the mixture is cooking gently but steadily. If the juices are a little thin, remove the tripe from the pot and reduce the liquid over high heat until it will coat the back of a spoon.

When ready to serve, stir in the remaining butter and the parmesan. Serve in deep, heated plates.

Serves 6-8

Lamb stew with red wine vinegar
Agnello in umido

With strongly flavored additions of red wine vinegar, anchovies and herbs, this Umbrian recipe is clearly an Etruscan legacy. In Umbria there's plenty of meat and the sheep here graze on lush meadows with beautiful wild herbs.

1½ tablespoons unsalted butter
3 tablespoons extra virgin olive oil
3 pounds boneless lamb shoulder, cut into 2-inch pieces
1 cup dry white wine
½ cup red wine vinegar
1 cup broth (see page 223)
4 large cloves garlic
2 anchovy fillets, drained
2 teaspoons rosemary leaves
soft polenta, to serve (see page 86)

In a large casserole, combine the butter and oil over moderately high heat and when the butter foam starts to subside, add the lamb, season with salt and pepper, and brown on all sides, about 6-8 minutes. Make sure the pan is not crowded, or do this in 2 batches.

Add the wine and simmer over low heat until wine has reduced by half, about 10 minutes. Add the vinegar and half of the broth and simmer gently, stirring from time to time, until the lamb is tender, about 1½ hours. If the pan becomes dry, add more of the broth.

Transfer the lamb to a large plate and keep warm. Combine the garlic, anchovy and rosemary on a board and chop finely together. Stir this mixture into the cooking liquid and simmer until slightly thickened, about 3-5 minutes. Check seasoning.

Spoon polenta in deep, heated plates, top with the lamb and the sauce and serve immediately.

Serves 6

Bread & Pizza

Bruschetta with chicken livers
Bruschetta con fegatini di pollo

Usually this chicken liver topping is served on crostini, but I prefer thicker, chewier and bigger bruschetta. If they're to go with drinks, I cut the toast in halves or quarters before adding the topping. As a starter, I serve them whole, with a fork and knife.

3 tablespoons extra virgin olive oil, plus extra, for the bruschetta
1 large onion, halved and thinly sliced
¼ cup dry white wine
½ large pickled gherkin, cut into pea-sized cubes
1 pound chicken livers, trimmed, rinsed and dried, cut into ½-inch pieces
pinch of sugar
4 thick slices country-type bread, such as *pane di casa*
1 large clove garlic, halved
1 heaped tablespoon chopped flat-leaf parsley

Combine the oil and onion in a pan and cook over moderate heat until soft, about 5 minutes, stirring frequently, adding the white wine little by little. Stir in the gherkin and cook another 5 minutes.

Preheat a broiler.

Turn the heat up to high, add the livers and sauté 3 minutes. Stir in sugar, salt and pepper, and sauté another 3 minutes, or until cooked through.

Meanwhile, toast the bread under the broiler on both sides. When cool enough to handle, rub hard on one side of the toast with the cut side of the garlic. Place the toast, garlic side up, on plates and drizzle with a little extra oil. Pile the livers on top, scatter with parsley, and serve immediately.

Serves 4

Bread, potato and arugula soup
Zuppa di pane, patate e rucola

Fabulously rustic, delightful and beautiful. Enough said!

2 cups pieces several-days-old Italian-type bread, such as *pane di casa,* crusts removed
1½ tablespoons extra virgin olive oil, plus 3 tablespoons extra
1 pound starchy potatoes, such as Yukon gold, peeled and cut into ½-inch thick slices
1 pound arugula (not baby arugula), tough stems removed, rinsed and cut into 2-inch pieces
6 large cloves garlic, chopped
1 whole dried red chili
½ cup freshly grated Pecorino Romano cheese

Preheat the oven to 350°F.

Combine the bread – just tear into pieces – in a large bowl with the oil and toss well to permeate all pieces. Spread on a baking sheet and toast in the oven until golden and crisp, about 15 minutes. Set aside.

Combine the potatoes and 7 cups water in a large pot, add salt and bring to a boil. Cook over moderately high heat and cook the potatoes, with lid set at an angle, until tender, but not falling apart, about 15-20 minutes. Add the arugula and reserved bread and cook another 10 minutes. The potato slices will start to break up.

Meanwhile, combine the extra 3 tablespoons oil, the garlic and chili in a small frying pan and cook over low heat until fragrant, about 5 minutes. Stir into the pot (remove the chili, if you like) and cook 1 minute more. Season with salt and pepper and serve in heated bowls. Serve with cheese at the table.

Serves 6

Baked bread and cabbage soup with fontina
Zuppa di pane e versa al forno

Save this to make on the next cool day and be ready for the fantastic cheesy fragrance to perfume your whole house. Good cheese and bread are the key to the success of this concoction, which is very similar to the French panade. As the finished product is not very soupy, I would recommend a bowl of extra, hot broth on the table, so people can help themselves, if they like.

3 tablespoons unsalted butter
½ savoy cabbage (about 2½ pounds), finely shredded
8 cups broth (see page 223)
pinch of freshly ground nutmeg
12 slices country-type Italian bread, such as *pane di casa*, toasted
1½ cups fontina or raclette cheese, coarsely chopped

Melt the butter over low heat in a large pot. Add the cabbage and season with salt. Place the lid securely on the pot and cook until the cabbage is tender, about 30 minutes, stirring from time to time.

Preheat the oven to 350°F. Place the broth in a pan and season with salt and pepper and a pinch of nutmeg. Bring to a simmer.

Place 4 slices of the toasted bread in an ovenproof pot or a deep, 16 cups capacity baking dish. Spoon half of the cabbage on top and then one third of the fontina. Make another layer of bread, the remaining cabbage and another one third of the cheese. Cover with the remaining bread and pour the simmering broth over all.

Scatter with the remaining cheese and bake until bubbling and browned on top, about 45 minutes. Remove from the oven and let stand 5 minutes. Bring a knife to the table to cut through the bread layers, to serve.

Serves 6

Bread and tomato salad
Panzanella alla toscana

There must be as many versions of this refreshing salad as there are households in Italy. This particular version was served to us in an age-old olive grove near Greve in Chianti. No cucumber or fancy additions here, basically just good bread, tomatoes and olive oil – the way it should be according to the Tuscans. There's no better way to use up stale bread – panzanella makes a satisfying starter on a hot summer night. It goes without saying that with so few ingredients, they should all be of absolute top quality; the tomatoes, especially, should be in their prime.

8 thick slices several-days-old Italian-style bread, such as *pane di casa* or ciabatta, crusts removed
1 cup tightly packed fresh basil leaves
1 red onion, halved lengthwise and cut into very thin slices
2 pounds ripe tomatoes, cored and coarsely chopped
¼ cup red wine vinegar
1½ tablespoons extra virgin olive oil

Place the bread in a bowl and cover completely with water. Let stand 10 minutes, then pick up handfuls of the bread and squeeze very gently, but thoroughly, between two cupped hands, until the bread is almost dry, but without crumbling it. Transfer the bread to a large bowl and discard the water.

Tear the basil leaves and add to the bread, together with the onion and tomatoes. Toss gently until well combined. Add vinegar and oil and toss again. The bread will now start to break into smaller pieces. Season with salt and freshly ground pepper. Refrigerate at least 1 hour before serving, but serve on the same day it's made.

Serves 6

Flatbreads
Crescente

These flatbreads are so easy to make, and for people who are unsure about working with yeast, there's none in this recipe. Crescente are nice to serve as a snack, just sprinkled with some sea salt and drizzled with oil as soon as they're cooked. Alternatively, they make a good starter, served with prosciutto, melon or figs, and big dollops of ricotta.

1 pound (3⅓ cups) all-purpose flour
1 teaspoon salt
⅛ teaspoon baking soda
1¼ cups milk
extra virgin olive oil, to cook

Combine the flour, salt, baking soda and milk in a large bowl and knead until smooth. Knead briefly on a lightly floured surface into a smooth ball, then wrap in a clean dish towel and refrigerate for 1 hour.

Tear off pieces and roll with your hands into walnut-sized balls, then roll the balls out on a lightly floured surface into 4- to 5-inch discs. Add a tablespoon of oil to a non-stick frying pan and fry the discs over moderate heat, one at a time, until golden and bubbly on both sides, about 2 minutes per side. Add more oil as necessary. Drain on paper towels and serve immediately, or allow to cool completely and store in an airtight container.

Serves 8

Three pizzas

This pizza dough is easy to make, especially if you have an electric mixer.
Semolina can be found in most health food stores and organic grocers.

Pizza dough (enough for 3 pizzas)
3 cups all-purpose flour
⅓ cup semolina
2 teaspoons salt
1½ cups warm water
¼ cup extra virgin olive oil
2 teaspoons dried yeast

To make the pizza dough, combine the flour, semolina and salt in a bowl of an electric mixer. Combine the water, oil and yeast in a small bowl and stir to dissolve yeast. Combine the 2 mixtures in the mixer bowl and mix with the beater until smooth, then change to the dough hook and mix at moderate speed for 10 minutes or until the dough is smooth and pliable. (If you don't have an electric mixer with a dough hook, knead by hand for 15-20 minutes.)

Oil a bowl, place the dough in the bowl and turn over to coat all sides with oil. Cover with plastic wrap and rest in a warm place until doubled in size (or overnight in the refrigerator).

Use the same method for each of the three pizzas. Preheat the oven to the highest possible setting. Roll ⅓ of the pizza dough on a well floured surface into a circle, place on an upside-down baking sheet covered generously with polenta, and put on chosen topping. The polenta acts like little ball bearings, making it easy to remove the pizza from the baking sheet.

Pizza with potato, pancetta and arugula
Pizza con patate, pancetta e rucola

dough for pizza base, rolled out (use ⅓ quantity, see above)
1½ tablespoons extra virgin olive oil, plus 1½ tablespoons extra
1 red potato, skin on, very thinly sliced (the best way is with a mandoline)
1 large clove garlic, finely chopped
1 teaspoon small rosemary sprigs
2 thin slices pancetta or prosciutto, cut into strips
handful baby arugula, well rinsed and spun dry

Brush the pizza base with 1½ tablespoons oil. Combine the extra tablespoon oil, potato, garlic and rosemary in a bowl, season with salt and pepper, and divide evenly over the pizza. Scatter with pancetta and bake for 10 minutes or until cooked through and the base is golden and crisp. Scatter with arugula and serve immediately.

(Continued next page)

Three pizzas

(Continued from previous page)

Artichoke pizza with goat's cheese
Pizza con carciofi

dough for pizza base, rolled out (use ⅓ quantity, see page 270)
¼ cup spreadable goat's cheese, plus ¼ cup extra
1 large artichoke, stem trimmed to 2 inches
1½ tablespoons extra virgin olive oil
2 large cloves garlic, finely chopped
¼ teaspoon chili flakes
handful thyme sprigs

Prepare the artichoke (see page 140). Cut artichoke into quarters, and cut each quarter into thin slices, including the stem, and return to acidulated water.

Combine oil, garlic and chili flakes in a frying pan and cook over moderate heat until fragrant, about 3 minutes. Drain the artichoke slices and stir into the pan. Season with salt and pepper, add ½ cup water and bring to a simmer. Cover with wet, crumpled parchment paper and simmer until artichoke is tender, about 10-15 minutes.

Spread ¼ cup goat's cheese on to the pizza base. Then arrange the artichoke slices over the pizza and scatter with thyme sprigs and small dollops of the goat's cheese. Bake in preheated oven until the pizza is brown and crisp, about 10 minutes. Serve immediately.

Pizza with tomatoes and basil
Pizza alla Margherita

⅓ quantity dough for pizza base, rolled out (use ⅓ quantity, see page 270)
1½ tablespoons extra virgin olive oil
1 large clove garlic, finely chopped
1½ tablespoons chopped fresh basil, plus 1½ tablespoons extra
4 roma tomatoes
1 ball fresh mozzarella cheese (about ¼ cup), sliced

Combine oil, garlic and basil in a small bowl and spread over the pizza. Cover with tomatoes and top with mozzarella. Bake in preheated oven until the pizza is brown and crisp, about 10 minutes. Serve immediately, scattered with extra basil.

Breadcrumbs

Bread is revered in Italy. Any stray piece dropped on the floor is picked up
– sometimes kissed – before being ceremoniously placed back on the cutting board,
and how right they are! Leftovers are used in salads, soups, puddings, cakes and
breadcrumbs. Italians make great bread, although the saltless bread of Tuscany
comes as a bit of a shock to most visitors.

BIG, FLUFFY BREADCRUMBS
To make big, fluffy breadcrumbs, leave an Italian-type loaf, such as ciabatta or *pane di casa*, out on the kitchen counter for a few days. Cut off the crust and cut into 2-inch pieces. Pulse in a processor until you have fluffy breadcrumbs, perfect to top gratins or to make into golden, crunchy crumbs for pasta if parmesan cheese is not available. Pack in freezer bags or containers and freeze for up to 6 months.

DRIED BREADCRUMBS
To make dried breadcrumbs, leave an Italian-type loaf, such as ciabatta or *pane di casa*, out on the kitchen counter for a few days. Remove the crusts and slice. Arrange on a baking sheet and place in a 275°F oven until the slices are light golden and completely dried out, about 15-20 minutes. Break into smaller pieces and grind in a processor until you have fine breadcrumbs. Transfer to an airtight jar and keep in a dry place for up to 3 months.

Sweet Things

Fig gratin
Fichi gratinati

Figs have been a mainstay of southern European cooking from the beginning of time. (Man has always had a love affair with figs, which were recorded as early as 3000 BC, and were present in the hanging gardens of Babylon.) I tend to associate figs, often accompanied by paper-thin slices of prosciutto, with endless summer lunches on shaded verandas in Italy or Greece, overlooking the Mediterranean. The fruit goes well with cooked savoury dishes, too, such as roast duck or pork, or wrapped in prosciutto and stuffed with cheese, especially goat's cheese or blue cheese. Figs are also used to make jam and tarts, as well as ice-cream.

In this simple recipe, the figs are merely heated and lightly sweetened with jam. A lovely ending to dinner, you can add a dollop of ice-cream or heavy cream.

8-12 ripe figs, halved
½ cup fig jam or raspberry jam
3 tablespoons grappa or brandy
1½ tablespoons brown sugar

Preheat oven to 350°F. Place the figs in a gratin dish, cut sides up.

Combine jam, grappa and sugar in a small pan and heat until bubbling. Pour mixture through a sieve, over the figs. Bake until the figs are heated through and the sauce is bubbling, about 8 minutes.

Serves 6

Milk pudding with strawberry sauce
Budino di latte

In areas where milk production is plentiful, such as Lombardy, the thrifty housewife often holds back some of the day's milking to make this pudding for her family at night. No eggs or butter, just milk thickened with potato flour. It looks deceptively like panna cotta, *but is so much lighter!*

4 cups milk
1 cup sugar
½ cup potato flour
1 cinnamon stick
1 vanilla bean, split

Strawberry sauce
1 pint strawberries, hulled and coarsely chopped
½ cup sugar
squeeze of lemon juice

Pour the milk in a saucepan and whisk in the sugar and potato flour until totally dissolved. Add the cinnamon and vanilla and bring to a boil. Reduce the heat to low and simmer, stirring constantly, until the mixture thickens to the consistency of thick cream, about 5-6 minutes.

Rinse a 5-cup mold with cold water and leave the inside wet (or divide among smaller molds). Pour in the pudding mixture and allow to cool to room temperature. Refrigerate until firmly set, about 3-4 hours or overnight.

To make the strawberry sauce, combine the strawberries, sugar and lemon juice in a saucepan and stir over moderate heat until the sugar has dissolved. Bring to a boil, then reduce heat and simmer 3 minutes. Pour into a bowl and allow to cool to room temperature. Refrigerate for 2 hours. Strawberry sauce may be made 1 day in advance.

To turn the puddings out of the mold(s), run a sharp knife around the inside rim and invert, then give the mold a hard tap. Serve with strawberry sauce.

Serves 8

Tiramisù

I have to admit I've never been a great fan of tiramisù (it means "pick-me-up"). The versions I've tried have always been too heavy and cloying for my taste. Not long ago I wanted to make this famous dessert for an Italian dinner in my classes, and it wasn't until I started experimenting for myself that I found the solution in the separate beating of the egg whites, folded into the mascarpone. The ladyfingers or savoiardi, drenched in coffee, are a much lighter alternative to the more usual sponge cake. It may be hard to believe, but this actually tastes very light.

3 large eggs, separated
1 cup sugar
2 cups mascarpone
3 tablespoons sweet Marsala
¼ cup grated dark chocolate
18-24 ladyfingers (savoiardi)
scant 1½ cups freshly made strong coffee, cooled to room temperature

Combine the egg yolks and sugar in a bowl and whisk until pale. Fold in the mascarpone. Beat the egg whites in a clean bowl until they form stiff peaks. Add Marsala and half of the grated chocolate. Whisk again until you have soft peaks. Fold gently into the mascarpone mixture.

Place a layer of ladyfingers to cover the bottom of a rectangular Pyrex dish. Pour half the coffee over the ladyfingers, soaking them well. Spread half of the mascarpone mixture on top, then make another layer with ladyfingers, coffee and mascarpone mixture. Sprinkle with remaining chocolate, then refrigerate at least 4 hours before serving.

Serves 6

Highs and lows
the faces of Rome

It was our friend's birthday and, deciding we'd celebrate in style, we booked a table at one of Rome's swankiest restaurants, a hotel penthouse, offering a panoramic view of the holy city by night, from the Villa Medici right up to the St. Peter's Duomo.

"Fine dining" isn't exactly my preferred style of eating, either at home or when I go out, so it was with a sinking feeling we went up in the lift at dizzying speed, having the distinct sensation we were going in the wrong direction. A trattoria would have been far more to my liking than the opulent room we were ushered into … but not before our friend, who was wearing an immaculate shirt but no tie, was outfitted with one a waiter supplied.

Our meal was duly served, starters, main course and dessert, every single dish without exception just as you would expect from a top-class kitchen in London, Paris or New York – unfortunately, there simply was nothing Roman, or even Italian about it. The main course was served with great fanfare, two waiters lifting the gleaming domes off our four plates in perfect harmony – not remotely a cucina povera *experience!*

For first-time visitors to Rome, the Vatican and the Forum and the Colosseum are musts. As the years and the visits have gone by, I've found that Rome has surprises that are much closer to home. Just inside the gates of the Piazza del Popolo is the unassuming façade of the church of Santa Maria del Popolo. It's the perfect place to sit down with your shopping and rest for a few minutes. And then you find you're looking at two magnificent Caravaggios in the gloom of the chapels ... On the steps of the same church I encountered another reality of Rome: street beggars – crouched figures of women, some with little children, with a begging cup held out. At Santa Maria del Popolo, one of the shrouded figures inadvertently looked up at me and, sadly, revealed herself as a bright-eyed young woman in her 20s ...

High on the agenda in Rome is eating and drinking, and although we're always keen to try new places, there are several that have stood the test of time. We return on a regular basis to restaurants such as La Rampa, tucked away under the Spanish steps, to join the scramble for a table at lunchtime, preferably outside when the weather allows – Romans like to work on their suntan at every opportunity. The food

is good, but predictable: there's a laden *antipasto* table inside, and every true Roman taste is on the menu. Traditions here die hard. Every Tuesday there's *Pasta and chickpea soup* (*Pasta e ceci*, see page 100), as dictated by the canonical calendar for generations. Of course, not everything stays the same around here, but try to ignore the nearby MacDonalds ... Across the piazza, in Via Mario de' Fiori you'll find Al 34, a cosy restaurant with time-honored specialties, such as braised pork or tripe. And pasta lovers can't do better than Gran Sasso in Via di Ripetta for the *Bucatini all'amatriciana*, long hollow pasta with a fiery tomato sauce with *guanciale* (pig's jowls and cheeks, like pancetta). Try their lamb, too.

For offal afficionados, the place to go is Testaccio, the home of *Quinto-Quarto* cooking. Offal accounts for a quarter of the whole weight of an animal (thus it was named the "fifth quarter") and has been enjoyed in the trattorias around the old slaughterhouse for centuries. The Mercato di Testaccio (food market) is much cheaper than the Campo dei Fiori, and I often go back for the *Saltimbocca alla romana* at Checchino dal 1887 in Via Monte Testaccio. Volpetti at Via Marmorate is great for some serious food shopping.

Limoncello ricotta soufflé
Soufflé di ricotta dolce

Especially for those who've never had the confidence to make soufflés, there's no reason why you shouldn't try your hand at these. The thick soufflé base is so stable, the egg whites merely come into the picture to lighten and lift! You can make your own almond meal by grinding blanched almonds in a nut mill or food processor until they reach the consistency of cornmeal.

unsalted butter, at room temperature, for soufflé dishes
sugar, for soufflé dishes
1½ cups fresh ricotta, drained
scant ½ cup sugar
scant ½ cup almond meal
3 tablespoons limoncello
5 large egg whites

Preheat the oven to 350°F, brush the insides of six, 1-cup capacity soufflé dishes with butter and coat with sugar, shaking out any excess.

Combine the ricotta, sugar, almond meal and limoncello in a bowl and stir until well incorporated. In a separate bowl, beat the egg whites until they hold stiff peaks. Stir a large spoonful of the egg whites into the ricotta to lighten the mixture, then fold in the remaining whites gently but thoroughly.

Spoon into the prepared soufflé dishes, filling them ¾ full, and bake 35 minutes or until well risen. Serve immediately.

Serves 6

Apple fritters
Fritelle di mele

There's no dessert more universally liked and reminiscent of childhood as good old apple fritters. This simple recipe from the Alto Adige region, which until after World War I was part of the Austrian Empire, are testament to Austria's love of all things sweet. Although the cuisine of Alto Adige could hardly be called pure Italian, this fritter recipe has become a staple dessert in winter in farmhouses all over Italy.

2 pounds apples, such as golden delicious or gala, peeled, cored and cut into ½-inch thick slices
¼ cup sugar
3 tablespoons grappa or brandy
4 eggs, separated
1½ cups milk
1½ tablespoons extra virgin olive oil, plus extra oil for deep frying
2 cups all-purpose flour
powdered sugar, to sprinkle

Combine the apple slices, sugar and grappa in a large bowl and toss to coat. Let stand for at least 2 hours at room temperature. Combine the egg yolks, milk, 1½ tablespoons oil, a pinch of salt and flour in a bowl and beat until smooth. Cover and refrigerate for 1-2 hours.

Beat the egg whites until they hold stiff peaks and fold lightly into the batter.

Pour 2 inches of the extra oil into a frying pan and heat to 350. Dip the apple slices, a few at a time, into the batter and slip into the hot oil. Fry until golden, turn over and fry until golden on both sides, about 3-4 minutes altogether. Transfer with a slotted spoon to paper towels.

Arrange the fritters on a heated platter and sprinkle with powdered sugar. Serve immediately.

Serves 6

Lemon rice cake
Torta di riso dolce

To end a summer meal, serve this delightfully light but slightly chewy cake, which is a cross between a sweet risotto and a souffle pudding. You can serve it soon after it comes out of the oven, but it's much easier to handle and cut neatly after it has been refrigerated a few hours or overnight.

unsalted butter, melted, and fine dried breadcrumbs, to coat a 8- to 9-inch springform cake tin
2½ cups milk
¾ cup arborio rice
¼ teaspoon salt
⅓ cup ground almonds
finely grated zest of 1 lemon
4 large eggs, separated
⅓ cup sugar
powdered sugar, to sprinkle

Preheat the oven to 400°F. Brush the cake tin liberally with butter, add breadcrumbs and rotate the tin in your hands to coat the inside all over. Shake to discard excess crumbs.

Bring the milk to a boil in a heavy-based pot and stir in the rice and salt. Reduce heat and simmer 10 minutes, stirring from time to time to ensure the rice doesn't stick to the bottom. Then start stirring constantly, until the rice has absorbed the milk, about another 10 minutes. Transfer to a bowl, allow to cool slightly, then stir in the almonds and lemon zest.

Beat the egg yolks lightly and gradually stir them into the rice mixture. Stir in the sugar. Beat the egg whites in a clean bowl until they form stiff peaks, then fold them gently into the rice mixture. Pour into the prepared cake tin and bake 30 minutes, or until a wooden skewer comes out clean. Let stand on a rack for 30 minutes, then run a sharp knife around the inside, release and remove the spring form, and slide cake on to the rack to cool completely. Sprinkle with powdered sugar and cut into wedges to serve.

Serves 8

Cherry walnut cake
Torta di ciliege e noci

When cherries are in season I love to make this cherry cake with its sweet-tart flavor and slightly crunchy top. Sometimes I make it in winter with morello cherries from a jar, which, quite apart from being widely available and easily stored in the pantry, have the added benefit of already being pitted. Also, beautiful frozen cherries can be found in supermarkets.

2 eggs, lightly beaten
1 cup sugar
1 teaspoon vanilla extract
1 cup all-purpose flour
1 teaspoon baking powder
½ teaspoon salt
¾ cup chopped walnuts
2 cups pitted cherries

Preheat the oven to 350°F. Butter a 9-inch round springform cake tin and line the bottom with parchment paper.

Combine the eggs, sugar and vanilla extract in a large bowl and beat until light. Sift the flour, baking powder and salt into another bowl and stir in the walnuts. Fold the flour mixture into the egg mixture, then fold in the cherries.

Pour the batter into the prepared cake tin, level the top and bake 1 hour and 20 minutes, or until a skewer comes out clean, and the top is golden. Remove to a wire rack to cool. To serve, cut into wedges.

Serves 8

Crumbly polenta cake
Torta sbrisolona

There's no better sweet, nibbly thing to have with a cup of coffee or tea than this polenta cake. Don't worry if the cake crumbles when cut, that's actually the whole idea of it. You can make your own almond meal by grinding blanched almonds in a nut mill or food processor until they reach the consistency of cornmeal.

heaping ⅓ cup almond meal
1 cup all-purpose flour
¾ cup polenta
scant 1 cup sugar
2 sticks unsalted butter, at room temperature
2 egg yolks
1 teaspoon vanilla extract
finely grated zest of 1 lemon
powdered sugar, for dusting

Preheat the oven to 350°F and line the bottom of a 9-inch springform cake tin with parchment paper.

Combine the almond meal, flour, polenta and sugar in a bowl and rub in the butter with your fingertips until the mixture resembles coarse meal.

Add the egg yolks, vanilla and lemon zest and knead briefly to combine. Press into the prepared cake tin and bake until the cake is golden brown, about 40-60 minutes. Remove the tin to a wire rack and cool 20 minutes. Remove the sides of the cake tin and dust with powdered sugar.

Serves 12

Frying pan apple cake
Torta di mele in padella

I guess it shouldn't come as a surprise that apples are frequently used in desserts, especially in rural areas where cellars are stocked with apples, pears, and root vegetables such as potatoes, to see families through cold winters. The texture of this cake is quite breadlike and goes well with a generous dollop of whipped cream.

3 tablespoons unsalted butter
4-5 golden delicious apples, peeled, cored and quartered
3 tablespoons brown sugar
heaping 1¾ cups all-purpose flour
3 teaspoons baking powder
2 large eggs
½ cup sugar
2 teaspoons vanilla extract
½ teaspoon ground cardamom
¾ cup milk
thick or whipped cream, to serve

Preheat the oven to 350°F.

Melt the butter in a heavy ovenproof or non-stick frying pan (measuring 9 inches across the top), over moderate heat, add the apples and fry until golden brown on all sides, about 10 minutes. Sprinkle with the brown sugar.

Sift the flour with the baking powder and a pinch of salt into a bowl. Combine the eggs with the sugar, vanilla extract, cardamom and milk in another bowl and whisk until smooth. Fold into the flour mixture until just combined.

Spoon over the apples in the frying pan and bake 30 minutes or until a skewer comes out clean. Turn out on to a flat plate and serve hot, with cream.

Serves 8

Flourless chocolate cake
Torta caprese

Graham Greene used to meet his friends and fellow writers, Shirley Hazzard, her husband Francis Steegmuller, and Gordon Douglas – on occasion accompanied by Elizabeth David – at the Gran Caffè in the Piazzetta in Capri, sometimes for coffee, or for drinks before dinner. All around, at cafes in the small, pretty piazza, people ate Torta caprese, *later made famous by its location and its illustrious visitors.*

1 stick unsalted butter
6 ounces dark chocolate, roughly chopped
1 cup sugar
5 large eggs, separated
1¼ cups finely ground almonds or hazelnuts, or a mixture of both
¼ teaspoon salt

Preheat the oven to 350°F and line a 9- to 10-inch springform cake pan with parchment paper. Butter the paper and sides of the pan.

Combine the butter, chocolate and sugar in a heatproof bowl and set over simmering water, making sure the bottom of the bowl does not touch the water. Heat until the butter is melted and the chocolate is soft, about 5 minutes. Remove from the heat and stir until the mixture is smooth. Cool to room temperature.

Beat the egg yolks into the chocolate mixture, one by one, with a wooden spoon, making sure each yolk is incorporated before adding the next. Stir in the almonds.

Beat the egg whites with the salt in a bowl until stiff peaks form. Fold into the chocolate mixture, one third at a time, just until no white streaks remain. Scrape into the prepared cake tin and bake 40-60 minutes, or until the cake starts to shrink away from the sides, and is firm in the middle, with a fudgy top. Cool on a rack. Remove the sides, then gently slide off the bottom and parchment paper on to a platter.

Serves 12

Lemon biscotti
Biscotti al limone

Sergio, the young Sicilian chef who gave me his recipe for linguine with calamari, garlic and lemon juice *(see page 44), let me into the secret of his grandmother's* biscotti. *Sicily is a rich source of lemons, so food using their precious juice and zest abounds, and can be either savoury or sweet. I love the way the little bits of zest become brittle while baking, giving an extra crunchy dimension. Serve these* biscotti *with morning coffee, afternoon tea, or after dinner with a glass of vin santo.*

3⅓ cups all-purpose flour
1 teaspoon baking powder
½ teaspoon salt
2 large eggs, at room temperature, plus 1 extra, for the egg wash
1 cup plus 3 tablespoons sugar
¼ cup extra light olive oil
peeled zest of 3 large lemons, finely chopped
½ cup milk

Preheat the oven to 350°F. Line 2 baking sheets with parchment paper.

Combine the flour, baking powder and salt and sift into a bowl. In the bowl of an electric mixer, whisk 2 eggs until foamy. Gradually add the sugar, whisking constantly, until the mixture is thick and very pale yellow, about 3-4 minutes. Whisk in the oil, and then the lemon zest.

Add the flour mixture, alternately with the milk, beginning and ending with flour. Transfer the dough to a well-floured surface and divide into 4 equal parts. Shape them into logs, about 1¼-inch thick. Use more flour, if necessary. Place the logs 2-inch apart on one of the prepared baking sheets. Mix the extra egg with 2 teaspoons water and brush over the logs. Bake until they are golden and firm, about 25 minutes, turning the baking sheet back to front halfway through baking time. Cool on the sheet on a wire rack for 10 minutes. Leave the oven on.

Using a bread knife, cut the logs diagonally into ½-inch thick slices. Lay the slices on the baking sheets and bake 15 minutes. Turn the slices over and bake another 15 minutes, or until the biscotti are golden on both sides. Cool on wire racks, then store in an airtight container.

Makes about 48

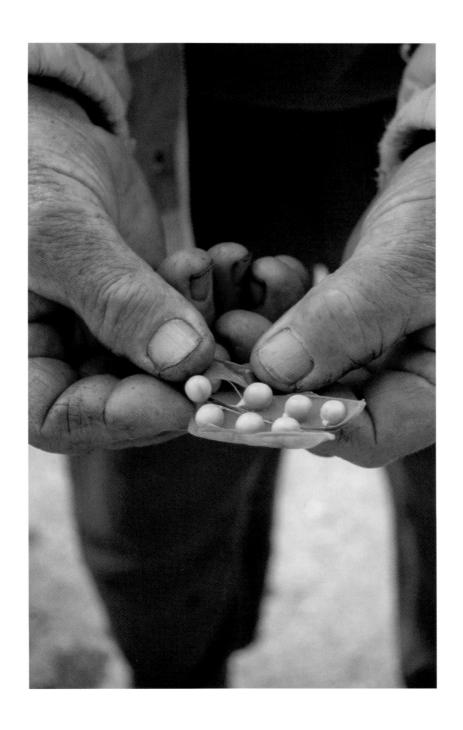

Simple utensils and really fresh food are the hallmark of cucina povera.
*Even the humblest ingredients, treated with loving care
(see* Risi e bisi, *page 64), can make a memorable meal. To repeat:
"The more you spend, the worse you eat."*

Index

Index